THE CIVILIZATION OF THE AMERICAN INDIAN SERIES

The Hasinais

THE HASINAIS

Southern Caddoans as Seen
by the Earliest Europeans

By

HERBERT EUGENE BOLTON

Edited and with an Introduction by

RUSSELL M. MAGNAGHI

UNIVERSITY OF OKLAHOMA PRESS : NORMAN

Library of Congress Cataloging-in-Publication Data

Bolton, Herbert Eugene, 1870–1953.
   The Hasinais, southern Caddoans as seen by the
earliest Europeans.

   (The Civilization of the American Indian series;
v. 182)
   Bibliography: p. 181.
   Includes index.
   1. Hasinai Indians.   2. Caddo Indians.   3. Indians
of North America—Texas.   I. Magnaghi, Russell M.
II. Title.   III. Series.
E99.H28B65   1987   976.4'00497   86–40525
ISBN 0–8061–2060–6 (alk. paper)

In Memory of
John Francis Bannon, S.J.
(1905–1986)
Friend and Mentor

Contents

Illustrations

MAP

Preface

The Hasinais is an ethnographic study of the Hasinai Indians of east Texas written by Spanish Borderlands historian Herbert Eugene Bolton. Although a historian, Bolton pioneered ethnography in this work, which has been widely praised by scholars. Unfortunately, owing to Bolton's busy schedule and a change in his research interest and focus, the work was never published.

Since the manuscript was first brought to my attention over a decade ago, my fondest dream has been to see it published and made available to the public. Not only is it Bolton's first monograph-length work, but it is also an excellent piece of ethnographic literature about a once important but little-known Indian tribe. I hope that the monograph will provide readers with new insights into the Hasinai way of life and aid scholars who are studying Caddoan archaeology, ethnography, and history.

Many people and institutions have provided me with invaluable assistance. The Bolton family gave me permission and encouragement to publish the manuscript. The Bancroft Library provided me with permission to copy, use, and publish the material. The Bancroft staff has always been helpful in my research endeavors. The same is true of the staffs of the Texas State Library, the University of Texas Library, and the Texas State Historical Association, all in Austin. Northern Michigan University provided me with a series of grants that allowed me to complete the research and editing of this work.

Over the years, especially when it seemed that work on the manuscript had come to a permanent halt, family members and friends provided essential encouragement. John Francis Bannon, S. J., who first brought the manuscript to my attention, frequently asked, "How's the Bolton manuscript coming along?" As a result of combined efforts, the work finally went to the publisher. To everyone, thank you; at last it is completed!

Marquette, Michigan   RUSSELL M. MAGNAGHI

The Hasinais

Editor's Introduction

The eminent historian Herbert Eugene Bolton (1870–1953) is best known for his work developing the study of the Spanish borderlands and the history of the Americas.[1] Close observation of his life and work indicates that Bolton was an ethnologist as well as a historian. His many translated works give the student of the American Indian new insights into aboriginal life and culture through Spanish documentation. During his publishing career, which began in 1902 at the University of Texas and ended after his retirement from the University of California in 1950, Bolton published more than eighty-five journal and popular articles and seventeen books, not to mention dozens of articles contributed to various encyclopedic works.[2] His papers in the Bancroft Library in Berkeley, California, verify that he had numerous projects that were never completed during his active lifetime.

One of these projects is a near-forgotten manuscript written during his early career, and its full story is as elusive as its subject, the Hasinai Indians of east Texas. The manuscript has remained in the Bancroft Library through the years, referred to on occasion but never published until now.

Bolton joined the faculty of the University of Texas in the fall of 1901 and found himself assigned to teach medieval his-

[1]John Francis Bannon, *Herbert Eugene Bolton: The Historian and the Man.*
[2]For a complete bibliography of Bolton's publications, see John Francis Bannon, ed., *Bolton and the Spanish Borderlands,* pp. 333–41.

tory. His academic career to that point did not indicate any interest in either the Indians or the Spaniards—his doctoral dissertation at the University of Pennsylvania was about antebellum blacks. George P. Hammond best described the change that took place while Bolton was in Austin:

Then came the great turning point in his life, his first real opportunity, when he accepted a position as instructor in history at the University of Texas. For the young professor, Texas opened new horizons. On every side were evidences of Spanish and Mexican civilization, people of a foreign tongue and of a Latin culture wholly different from that of Middle Western United States.[3]

Bolton realized that there was a great gap in scholarship in American history, which usually began with the arrival of the English colonists and all but ignored the Spaniards, who had arrived and settled much earlier.

This new awareness and interest led Bolton to study the Spanish language as a prerequisite to reading the largely untouched documents. He dug into the Bexar Archives in the university, and he went off to the Archivo General of Mexico. This activity led to the publication of a number of important articles in the *Quarterly* of the Texas State Historical Association, among them "Some Materials for Southwestern History in the Archivo General de Mexico" (October, 1902, and January, 1904), "Tienda de Cuervo's Ynspección of Laredo, 1757" (January, 1903), and the long article "The Spanish Abandonment and Re-Occupation of East Texas, 1773–1779" (October, 1905).[4]

[3] George P. Hammond. "Herbert Eugene Bolton, 1870–1953," *Americas* 9 (April, 1953): 392.
[4] Herbert Eugene Bolton, "De Los Mapas," *Quarterly* of the Texas State Historical Association 6 (July, 1902): 69–70; "Some Materials for Southwestern History in the Archivo General de Mexico," ibid., 6 (October, 1902): 103–12, and 7 (January, 1904): 196–213; "Tienda de Cuervo's Ynspección of Laredo, 1757," ibid., 6 (January, 1903): 187–203; and "The Spanish Abandonment and Re-Occupation of East Texas, 1773–1779," ibid., 9 (October, 1905): 67–137.

4

Bolton soon discovered that disciplines other than history must be learned to understand the story he was endeavoring to tell. He became acutely aware that American history had always involved the Indians and that, as he began to study southwestern history, he also had to study the ethnology of the region. As he searched through the available studies, he found that they were largely English in their documentation. He discovered in his work with the Spanish documents that they shed new light on the history not only of the region but also of the Indians and their culture. He found that bits of extinct Indian languages could be reconstructed from the Spanish records. As a result Bolton the historian became Bolton the ethnologist.[5]

While Bolton was busy in Texas carving out a whole new field of study, the Smithsonian Institution's Bureau of American Ethnology was developing an encyclopedic two-volume work, *The Handbook of American Indians North of Mexico.* The volumes were inspired by the chief of the bureau, W. H. Holmes and edited by Frederick Webb Hodge. Bolton had seen a brief notice concerning this project and on January 8, 1906, wrote to the bureau seeking more information and offering his services.[6] Thus began Bolton's association with the bureau, an association that eventually led to his work on the Hasinai Indians.

[5] Bolton, "How I Got That Way," MS in Bolton Papers, part 2, "Out," The Bolton Papers are in the Bancroft Library, Berkeley, California. The collection dates from 1906. The papers are divided into three parts, the second of which contains Bolton's correspondence, identified as "In" and "Out." I have used this correspondence extensively, and if a notation is not given in the notes, it can be assumed that the item is from this body of correspondence. Much original and duplicate correspondence between Bolton and Bureau of American Ethnology personnel—Holmes, Hodge, and Swanton—can also be found in the files of the National Anthropological Archives (hereafter NAA), Smithsonian Institution; Russell M. Magnaghi, "Herbert E. Bolton and Sources for American Indian Studies, "*Western Historical Quarterly* 6 (January, 1975): 33–46.

[6] Bolton to J. W. Powell, January 8, 1906, NAA.

On Hodge's advice Holmes wrote to Bolton on January 18 seeking his assistance and expertise on the Texas Indians. By this date the first volume was nearing completion, but Holmes felt that Bolton's work would be an asset for the second volume. Pages from the publication were sent for Bolton's inspection along with an apology that funds for compensation were not available.[7] Bolton's reply was accompanied by the revised pages that he had corrected with readily available information. He expressed regret that he was extremely busy and did not have time to do a more thorough job. At this time Bolton was primarily interested in eighteenth-century Texas, but he realized that a study of earlier material would add greatly to knowledge of the Indian tribes of Texas. He was extremely disappointed that the bureau editors, working with the Texas Indians, had used only the Nacogdoches Archives in the state library rather than the more extensive Bexar Archives.[8]

As the weeks passed, Bolton was gradually drawn into the bureau's *Handbook.* On February 6 he wrote that he did not have time to work on a detailed study but added, "If I have time, I am sure that I could find a great detail of interesting and important information in our rich collection of manuscripts."[9] He continued to send back to Washington valuable notes, and Holmes quickly saw the value of Bolton and his information.

As word of Bolton's knowledge of the Texas Indians began to spread throughout the Bureau of Ethnology, anthropologist John R. Swanton sought his assistance. Swanton was interested in the Indian tribes that had become or were becoming extinct in Texas and especially in Louisiana.[10] In 1906 he was having trouble locating small tribes in Louisiana but stated

[7]W. H. Holmes to Bolton, January 18, 1906, Bolton Correspondence, "In."

[8]Bolton to Holmes, January 25, 1906, Bolton Correspondence, "Out."

[9]Bolton to Holmes, February 6, 1906, Bolton Correspondence, "Out."

[10]John R. Swanton's research on the Louisiana Indians was published as *Indian Tribes of the Lower Mississippi Valley and Adjacent Coast of the Gulf of Mexico,* Bureau of American Ethnology Bulletin no. 43 (1911).

that the problem was even greater with the Texas Indians—
that "it appears infinitely worse especially along the coast,
where, with the exception of a few prominent tribes, no two
lists seem to agree."[11] Swanton sought Bolton's expertise to
aid him in the identification and location of tribes in Louisiana and Texas and in the determination of their linguistic
stocks through the use of French and Spanish documents.
During the greater part of 1906 the two scholars, far removed
from one another, were in correspondence concerning Indian
matters.

Holmes saw the possibilities of using Bolton's knowledge for
more than the contributions in the *Handbook*. At this early
juncture in their relationship Holmes proposed a monograph
on the history of the Indian tribes of Texas. He was quick to
point out that this was not a definite contract offer because
funds for fiscal 1906 had already been allocated but said that
1907 looked promising. Holmes did not place any restriction
on the monograph and asked Bolton to offer suggestions on
length, reasonable compensation, and approximate completion date.[12] On the same day Swanton wrote about other
matters and offered Bolton help in the publication of the
Texas Indian monograph upon its completion.[13] The first over-
ture was made that would lead not to the proposed Texas Indian monograph but to the Hasinai manuscript. It was a few
days before Bolton could give the bureau a "clear decision."[14]

During the latter half of February, Bolton thought about the
proposal while in the midst of a busy teaching schedule and his
work on his *Guide to Materials for the History of the United
States in the Principal Archives of Mexico*.[15] In a letter to Holmes
dated March 1, he agreed to go ahead with the project, which

[11] Swanton to Bolton, February 12, 1906, Bolton Correspondence, "In."
[12] Holmes to Bolton, February 12, 1906, Bolton Correspondence, "In."
[13] Swanton to Bolton, February 12, 1906, Bolton Correspondence, "In."
[14] Bolton to Swanton, February 12, 1906, Bolton Correspondence, "Out."
[15] For a complete study of Bolton and the *Guide*, see John Francis Bannon, "Herbert E. Bolton: His *Guide* in the Making," *Southwestern Historical
Quarterly* 73 (July, 1969): 35–55.

he figured would run to approximately 150,000 words. Bolton the historian stressed that the bureau should expect not an anthropological work but one of a historical nature:

My idea would be to examine minutely the location, culture and inter-relations of the tribes at the earliest discovery. This done, I should wish to trace out these relations with the Spanish and French (of Louisiana, who had great influence in Texas), and later with the Anglo-Americans; the effects of these relations upon the natives; inter-tribal relations and tribal movements during contact with Europeans and Americans; and finally, the removal of the tribes to reservations. It would be desirable to include a study of archaeological remains, but I do not suppose much could be done in this direction in the near future.[16]

He believed that he could have the work finished within a year but that it would very likely take double the time because of research trips to Mexico and Washington, D.C. He could begin work immediately with the Bexar Archives, his private manuscripts, and the available printed sources. Holmes was pleased with Bolton's acceptance, and the project was under way.

The project quickly gained momentum, and by March 28 Bolton was looking forward to his summer research trip to Mexico. He sought money to employ readers in the Bexar Archives to save time and spare his eyes.[17] By mid-April he was in the midst of his work and needed publications that the bureau could send him. In a letter to Swanton he stressed the historical nature of the project and his intention to leave linguistic analysis to an expert.[18] At the same time Bolton continued to contribute to the *Handbook*. In June and July Bolton compiled a bibliography of the materials available in Austin, to avoid unnecessary expenditures of time and money in Mexico.

With the start of the new fiscal year Bolton wrote to Holmes

[16] Bolton to Holmes, March 1, 1906, Bolton Correspondence, "Out."
[17] Bolton to Holmes, March 11, 1906, Bolton Correspondence, "Out."
[18] Bolton to Swanton, April 18, 1906, Bolton Correspondence, "Out."

seeking definite confirmation on the project and compensation. If he had not received an answer by the time he left for Mexico, he said, he planned to drop the idea.[19] Holmes immediately responded that $1,000 had been allocated and that it would be paid by check on receipt by the bureau of the first half of the proposed monograph. However, under government regulations, Bolton would have to wait for travel, subsistence, and copying expenses, since reimbursement could be made only if the bureau purchased the completed manuscript.[20]

Bolton modified his plans for the original study on the Texas Indians, for the subject had proved to be too extensive to be covered in a single work. It had to be divided and published along regional lines. Under these modified plans Bolton concentrated his efforts on the Hasinai Indians of east Texas. It was his conviction that to understand Spanish Indian policy one first had to understand the Indian culture.[21] Bolton intended to describe Hasinai society in considerable detail in a section that could well develop into a paper of 25,000 words or more. At this time Bolton outlined the paper, indicating that he had the topic under control. He meant to include a general description of the Hasinai country, data on their name, and the tribes' locations and population, economic organization, art and architecture, social patterns, and religious and military customs. On August 6, Holmes sent an encouraging letter stressing that the emphasis on the Hasinais would not be out of proportion to the rest of the work.[22]

In the late summer of 1906, Bolton traveled south into Mexico and obtained a great quantity of material on the Texas Indians in addition to his *Guide* research. Upon his return work on the *Handbook* proceeded at great speed. Holmes was glad that Bolton could find time to rewrite and revise the *Handbook* material, for which Bolton was paid the usual

[19] Bolton to Holmes, July 19, 1906, Bolton Correspondence, "Out."
[20] Holmes to Bolton, July 23, 1906, Bolton Correspondence, "In."
[21] "Notes for the Hasinai," Bolton Papers, part 3, carton 23.
[22] Holmes to Bolton, August 6, 1906, Bolton Correspondence, "In."

cyclopedia rate of $10 per 1000 words. The editor, Hodge, was also pleased with Bolton's work and expected to use material for the first volume in a second revised edition. Bolton sent the bureau photographs of the Texas missions, and he was encouraged to collect photographs for his own monograph.

The Hasinai portion of the project was also progressing well. By April, 1907, Hodge was so encouraged that he wrote that it had "practically reached the final stage."[23] On June 3, in a progress report of the material submitted by Bolton, we see its direction:

While I did not approach this portion of the task with the equipment of a professional ethnologist, I have been about to put together a large amount of cultural data concerning these people [Hasinai] that has been hitherto unorganized and mainly unknown, and which it appeared to me should be presented as an introduction to the narrative history of the group. In writing this sketch I have made it very detailed and it may need compression before publication.[24]

It is evident from his report that he planned to write an introduction dealing with Hasinai culture, to be followed by a historical account of these people and their contact with white men. In the same report, concerning the Texas Indian project in general, Bolton wrote:

The task of writing the history of the Texas tribes is a gigantic one, and can be performed only by long and painful effort, but its successful accomplishment promises much addition to our knowledge of the native Americans.[25]

While in Mexico in the autumn of 1907, Bolton and Holmes continued to discuss the length of the project and payment for it. For budgetary reasons Bolton was asked to submit revised plans for the entire monograph. The original plan had called for the work to be in two parts, with Bolton paid at

[23] Frederick W. Hodge to Bolton, April 23, 1907, Bolton Correspondence, "In."

[24] Bolton to Holmes, June 3, 1907, Bolton Correspondence, "Out."
[25] Ibid.

Herbert Eugene Bolton ca. 1907, at the time he wrote the Hasinai manuscript. Courtesy Bancroft Library, University of California at Berkeley.

the rate of $13.33 per 1,000 words. The revised plan called for several manuscripts, which would be assembled along geographical lines or according to related tribes. Holmes was elated that the Hasinai manuscript, at 40,000 words, was nearly completed and was eager to have it ready for publication by July 1, 1908.

The title of the Hasinai monograph began to cystallize in 1907. The first title was rather long and descriptive: "The Hasinai Indians of the Neches-Angelina Valleys at the Coming of the Spaniards and the French." This was soon changed to the more colorful "Red Men of the Piney Woods [penciled in by Bolton on the original]: The Hasinai at the Coming of the Spaniards." In later years the manuscript was referred to as "The Hasinai at the Coming of the Europeans." The present title is a modification of these developments.

By late November, 1907, the Hasinai work was in a new phase. Bolton saw it as an introduction to a historical survey of the Hasinais. Because the entire work could not be finished by the July 1, 1908, deadline, Bolton proposed that the introduction could be issued separately, followed by the historical development, without impairing the value of the work.[26] In mid-December, Holmes wrote back, anticipating that the first part of the Hasinai work would be finished. He suggested that it appear in either the Bureau of American Ethnology's *Reports* or its *Bulletin*, depending on the status of publication at the time. Bolton was also contemplating publication of a separate article on the Hasinais and sought Holmes's approval. It was given, with the provision that the article would not deprive the bureau publication of any scholarly credit.[27]

Through the summer of 1908, Bolton was deeply involved in a Mexican archival project for the Carnegie Institution,

[26] Bolton to Holmes, November 27, 1907, NAA.
[27] Holmes to Bolton, December 13, 1907, Bolton Correspondence, "In." The only portion of the manuscript to be published is in "The Native Tribes About the East Texas Missions," *Quarterly* of the Texas State Historical Association 11 (April, 1908): 249–76.

and he could do little work on the Hasinai manuscript or the Texas project. Holmes continued to badger him and on April 15 wanted to know if the project could be submitted for publication by June 30. Monies had to be allocated to other projects; Bolton would not lose his money, Holmes assured him, but payment would have to wait until completion of the manuscript.[28] By June 17, Bolton still had not sent the manuscript; Holmes, always pleasant, stated that he was not inconvenienced by this delay.[29]

At this point the correspondence between Bolton and the bureau began to diminish. In the early spring of 1909, Hodge wrote to Bolton "very anxious to know" for the next fiscal year how the plans for the Texas tribes project were proceeding. He expressed hope that Bolton could send the material soon; otherwise the money allocated for it would be used in other projects.[30] There is no reason given in Bolton's correspondence why the manuscript on the Hasinais was not submitted for publication. But the original 1907 copy remained in rough state and certainly needed revision. This would have taken time to accomplish, and Bolton was involved in other projects and was contemplating a move westward.

The year 1909 was a turning point in Bolton's career and interests. He resigned from the University of Texas and in the fall began teaching at Stanford University. With the shift in geographic location gradually came a shift of Bolton's emphasis from the Spaniards in Texas to their countrymen on the West Coast and in California. Holmes sensed this change in interests and hoped that if Bolton could finish the "southwestern work you have already undertaken" and then get on with the California material "we will feel more reconciled." He continued, "Please let me know sometime if you think you will be able to prepare the monograph on the history of the Indians in Texas, or whether, in view of your *Handbook* ar-

[28] Holmes to Bolton, April 15, 1908, Bolton Correspondence, "In."
[29] Holmes to Bolton, June 17, 1908, Bolton Correspondence, "In."
[30] Hodge to Bolton, March 22, 1909, Bolton Correspondence, "In."

ticles, you now consider it desirable to do so."[31] The first attempts to get the Hasinai manuscript into print had ended in
failure, but only through Bolton's own reluctance.

For the next two years Bolton was busy with his teaching at
Stanford and with other research projects. Early in 1911,
L. W. Payne, of the University of Texas, was establishing the
Texas Folklore Society and sought Bolton's aid concerning Indian folklore. In response to this request Bolton spent considerable time developing a detailed program entitled "Suggestions for a Program for the Study of the Indian Folklore of
Texas." In a letter to Payne, Bolton wrote that he would be
interested in presenting a paper that was a long chapter from
the Hasinai manuscript, "Religious Beliefs and Customs of the
Hasinai."[32] At the first meeting of the new society on April 8,
1911, Bolton's work was read in absentia to the assembled
group on the University of Texas campus. Bolton had hoped
that the paper would be published, but it never was.

The Hasinai and Texas Indian project had apparently been
all but forgotten. Bolton failed to mention it in a congratula-
tory letter to Hodge upon completion of the *Handbook* in
early 1911.[33] Bolton was immersed in other projects and by
September was working seriously on the future *Athanase de
Mézières and the Louisiana-Texas Frontier*.[34] In 1914, Hodge
wrote to Bolton hoping to persuade him to revive the original
Texas Indian project with the assistance of John R. Swanton
and James Mooney, but to no avail. A brief look at Bolton's
publications during these years at the University of California
gives a clear indication of his interests. The Texas Indians
were not among them, and once again the Hasinai project was
dropped and forgotten.[35]

---

[31] Hodge to Bolton, February 2, 1910, Bolton Correspondence, "In."

[32] Bolton to L. W. Payne, February 12, 1911, Bolton Correspondence,
"Out."

[33] Bolton to Hodge, February 17, 1911, Bolton Correspondence, "Out."

[34] Bolton to Arthur H. Clark, September 4, 1911, Bolton Correspondence, "Out."

[35] Bannon, *Bolton and the Spanish Borderlands*, pp. 335–38.

In the late 1920s the Hasinai project was again revived. Alfred L. Kroeber, professor of anthropology in the University of California and a good friend of Bolton's, agreed to read the Hasinai manuscript. On January 17, 1927, Kroeber returned it with a note that it was a valuable piece of work and that he would proudly have it published at the University of California Press as soon as possible.[36] The manuscript still had not been published by October, when Swanton wrote Bolton to encourage him to submit his work on the "Caddo dialect," indicating that Swanton knew of it but had never read it.[37] A month later Swanton wrote, "As to the Caddo paper, I am willing to bet that you are the only living man capable of improving on it"[38] In the early summer of 1928, Swanton again sought to persuade Bolton to have the manuscript published.[39] But as the decade ended, it remained in its original typed form, and publication had been put off for the future. It must be remembered that during the late 1920s Bolton was deeply involved with a number of major publications: *Historical Memoirs of New California by Fray Francisco Palou, O.F.M.* (1926), *Fray Juan Crespi, Missionary, Explorer on the Pacific Coast, 1769–1774* (1927), *History of the Americas: A Syllabus with Maps* (1928), and the five-volume work *Anza's California Expedition* (1930). Little time was left for the revival of the Hasinai project, let alone the massive Texas Indian project.

Bolton's active scholarly life continued throughout the 1930s with the publication of *Font's Complete Diary* (1931), *The Padre on Horseback* (1932), and the *Rim of Christendom* (1936). Additional effort went into the writing of articles and his presidential address, "The Epic of Greater America," before the American Historical Association in 1932.

Once again, as in the 1920s, the Hasinai project made its way to the surface. In 1936, Leslie Spier, anthropologist at

[36] Alfred L. Kroeber to Bolton, January 17, 1927, Bolton Correspondence, "In."
[37] Swanton to Bolton, October 7, 1927, Bolton Correspondence, "In."
[38] Swanton to Bolton, November 2, 1927, Bolton Correspondence, "In."
[39] Swanton to Bolton, June 14, 1928, Bolton Correspondence, "In."

Yale University, tried to get Bolton interested in publishing it. He had met Bolton during the 1920s when Spier was acting curator of the University of California Museum of Anthropology (1920), research associate (1923), and visiting professor at Berkeley.[40] Sometime while Spier was at Berkeley, Bolton asked him to read the manuscript to get his impressions. Spier strongly urged Bolton to publish it. Spier wrote in late October, 1936, that after "all of these years it was lain in my mind as an important contribution which should see the light," stressing that its appearance would be of vital importance to American anthropology. The Yale anthropologist saw its major value as a representation of an Indian culture common to the southeastern United States that flourished as far west as the Angelina and Trinity valleys. Spier wanted to publish the work in the Memoirs of the American Anthropological Association, of which he was editor. If this proposal did not interest Bolton, there was a second possibility: through the Hodge Anniversary Publication Fund there was money available for two volumes in 1937. However, Spier preferred publication in the Memoirs because of its wider circulation.[41] Bolton did not reply to this inquiry, and nearly a year later Spier wrote again concerning possible publication. Spier stressed the importance of the work and asked Kroeber to press Bolton to prepare it for publication.[42]

Finally Bolton replied on October 27, 1937, saying that he was pleased by Spier's earlier letters but was so involved in research and teaching that, although he favored the suggestion, needed time to consider it.[43] During 1937, Bolton was extremely busy with numerous projects. In early February, Sir Francis Drake's plate of brass had been discovered; during the

[40] Sherwood L. Washburn, acting chairman of anthropology, to Dean Morris A. Stewart, Berkeley campus, July 12, 1960. Spier Papers, Department of Anthropology, University of California, Berkeley.

[41] Spier to Bolton, October 28, 1936, Bolton Correspondence, "In."

[42] Spier to Bolton, October 13, 1937, Bolton Correspondence, "In."

[43] Bolton to Spier, October 27, 1937, Bolton Correspondence, "Out."

following months Bolton verified its authenticity and joyfully announced it at a meeting of the California Historical Society. In May and June he traveled to the East and the Southwest, receiving honorary degrees from Marquette University and the University of New Mexico. Later in the summer, as a member of the National Park Service Advisory Board, he visited the Purisima Mission reconstruction project at Lompoc, California, and on September 1 and 2 he was in Saint Louis surveying the Jefferson Memorial. Only a week or two before his departure for Peru, he was busily preparing for the December Lima Conference that removed him from Berkeley for two months. A good portion of 1938 was spent catching up on work that had collected while he was gone.[44]

Spier grew anxious concerning Bolton's manuscript and spent 1938 trying to get him to publish it. On January 18, Spier was still waiting for the definitive answer promised in October.[45] Not hearing from Bolton, Spier sent him a telegram on February 15 requesting an immediate decision on the Hasinai. Still without an answer a week later, Spier informed Bolton that the Hasinai manuscript would have to be published later.[46] Finally Bolton replied apologetically in March that he was too busy to look over the manuscript.[47] Spier responded on March 17, glad to find Bolton still interested and stressing that publication money was still available and urging him to send the manuscript at his earliest convenience.[48] By October the revised manuscript had not arrived, though Spier remained interested.[49] Internal evidence shows that the original 1907 work was revised, retyped, and prepared for publication. The changes from the earlier manuscript were minor.

[44] Bannon, *Herbert Eugene Bolton*, pp. 198–211.
[45] Spier to Bolton, January 18, 1938 and February 15, 1938, Bolton Correspondence, "In."
[46] Spier to Bolton, February 22, 1938, Bolton Correspondence, "In."
[47] Bolton to Spier, March 12, 1938, Bolton Correspondence, "Out."
[48] Spier to Bolton, March 17, 1938, Bolton Correspondence, "In."
[49] Spier to Bolton, October 10, 1938, Bolton Correspondence, "In."

Correspondence in the Bolton papers does not indicate why it was not published at this time.

In 1939, Bolton began to have second thoughts about making public this valuable piece of anthropology. He felt that since he first wrote the manuscript new material unfamiliar to him had appeared and his work would have to be revised. He was ready to turn the whole project over to Alfred Kroeber to have it edited and published.[50] However, the manuscript was never sent to Kroeber. This was the last time the idea of publication of the Hasinai manuscript was contemplated for many years.

Bolton never lost interest in the Hasinai Indians. In 1940 he wrote that he was not doing any research on the subject but hoped to return to it "as my first love at no distant date."[51] This desire was never realized, but a portion of the original Hasinai project was completed by a student. William J. Griffith worked under Bolton at the University of California and in 1942 finished his thesis, "The Spanish Occupation of the Hasinai Country, 1690–1737." Using Bolton's data, Griffith briefly surveyed the ethnology of the Hasinais and then concentrated on their interaction with the Spaniards.

Until 1950, Bolton continued to send material on the Texas Indians to persons who requested it. In response to a letter from G. Sjoberg, of the Department of Sociology in the University of Texas, he wrote: "The most fruitful of my Texas studies, from an ethnological point of view, dealt with the Orcoquiza, Bidai, and Hasinai areas, not all of which data got into the *Handbook*."[52] This was the last correspondence in which Bolton that mentioned the Hasinais. The manuscript remained unpublished after three unsuccessful attempts.

---

[50] Bolton to Winnie Allen, July 26, 1939, Bolton Correspondence, "Out."

[51] Bolton to Dr. Albert Woldert, February 6, 1940, Bolton Correspondence, "Out."

[52] Bolton to G. Sjoberg, September 21, 1950, Bolton Correspondence, "Out."

From Bolton's death in 1953 until the present publication, little was done with the original manuscript, which remained in the Bolton Papers in the Bancroft Library. In 1954, Bolton's former student, William J. Griffith, published *The Hasinai Indians of East Texas as Seen by Europeans, 1687–1772.* Griffith was the first to admit that the original Bolton work was the superior: "The most complete and authoritative study of Hasinai ethnology is an unpublished manuscript of 183 typewritten pages of Herbert E. Bolton, entitled, 'The Hasinai Indians on the Coming of the Europeans.'"[53] That appears to be the only time the original manuscript was cited in a bibliography.

During the late 1960s and 1970s John Francis Bannon, S.J., spent his summer vacations at the Bancroft Library preparing a biographical study of his former mentor, Bolton. In the process of going through the many boxes that comprise the Bolton Papers, Bannon discovered the unpublished manuscript on the Hasinai Indians. Later he wrote concerning the possible publication of the piece:

The publication of the Hasinai story would add much to the Bolton total works. Colleagues and later folk knew of his interest in the Texas Indians but had nothing more of his works or thought save the many short articles in the *Handbook of American Indians North of Mexico.*[54]

Bannon brought this discovery to my attention, commenting that the publication of the manuscript would be "a real contribution."

Armed with a research grant from Northern Michigan University, I traveled to Berkeley in the summer of 1971 and began working with the manuscript. Permission to publish the

---

[53] William J. Griffith, *The Hasinai Indians of East Texas as Seen by Europeans, 1687–1772,* p. 58.

[54] John F. Bannon, "The Hasinai Manuscript of Herbert Eugene Bolton," September 9, 1978, MS in the possession of the editor.

work was given by the director of the Bancroft Library and the Bolton family.

Because this was Bolton's first major monographic study, from the inception of this undertaking I took the position that the integrity and style of the original work must be scrupulously maintained. This position was bolstered by the fact that over the years a number of Bolton's colleagues had read the manuscript and encouraged him to publish it as it was written. A careful reading of the piece indicated that its conclusions remained valuable.

Some editing of a minor nature had to be carried out on the manuscript. Repetitious sections and unnecessary insertions that had found their way into the work over the years were removed, and a number of emendations were made. A major change was the division of Bolton's extremely long chapter on Economic Life into two chapters, 4 and 5.

Other major improvements and changes concentrated in the footnotes and the bibliography. The footnotes proved to be incomplete, and the necessary information was sought out. This proved to be a task to tax the skill of a detective, but the resources of the University of California Libraries met the challenge. Spanish documentation was checked, and footnote style was clarified. For instance, Bolton's use of the term "Memorias" is outdated and did not coincide with the modern usage of "Historia" in describing a portion of the archival material from Archivo General de la Nación (A.G.N.) in Mexico City. Furthermore, it should be noted that all the Spanish documents cited throughout the manuscript have been copied or microfilmed and are readily available to researchers in American libraries such as the Bancroft Library at the University of California, Berkeley, and at the Center for Studies in Texas History at the University of Texas at Austin. Part or all of the documents have been translated, edited, and published in various books and articles over the years. Since the original manuscript did not include a bibliography, one was constructed from the corrected and modernized footnote data.

As a result of this editing, the original Bolton manuscript has been prepared much as Bolton would have envisioned it, supplemented with appropriate illustrations and maps. Now, after more than eighty years, Bolton's first major monograph reaches publication.

The Hasinais

I

The Hasinais

Of the native tribes who at the opening of historical times lived between the lower Red River and the Pecos, a stretch of six hundred miles, those having the highest civilization were the Caddos, a people who occupied the northeastern corner of Texas and adjacent territory on the left banks of the Red River. They belonged to the Caddoan linguistic stock, a large family which comprised three principal geographic groups. These divisions were the northern, represented by the Arikaras of North Dakota; the middle, which included the Pawnee confederacy, formerly living on the Platte River of Nebraska and to the west and southwest thereof; and the southern, embracing most of the tribes of the northeastern fourth of Texas, together with many bands of southern Arkansas and Oklahoma and of western Louisiana.[1]

Of the southern group the Caddos were socially the most advanced, as they have been historically the most important. Although they have been treated as a single confederacy and are known to ethnologists by a common name, a close study shows that they were sharply subdivided geographically and, it seems quite probable, organically, into two or more groups. One of these divisions, the southernmost, occupied a compact and somewhat isolated area in the middle Neches and upper

[1] J. W. Powell, *Indian Linguistic Families of America North of Mexico,* Seventh Annual Report of the Bureau of American Ethnology, p. 182 and map; Frederick W. Hodge, ed., *Handbook of American Indians North of Mexico,* Bureau of American Ethnology Bulletin no. 30 (1907), 1:182.

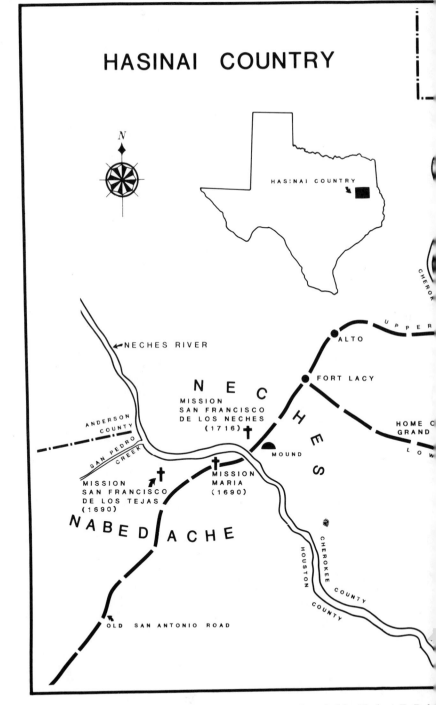

Locations of the Hasinai settlements, 1690–1790, as identified by Herbert E. Bol

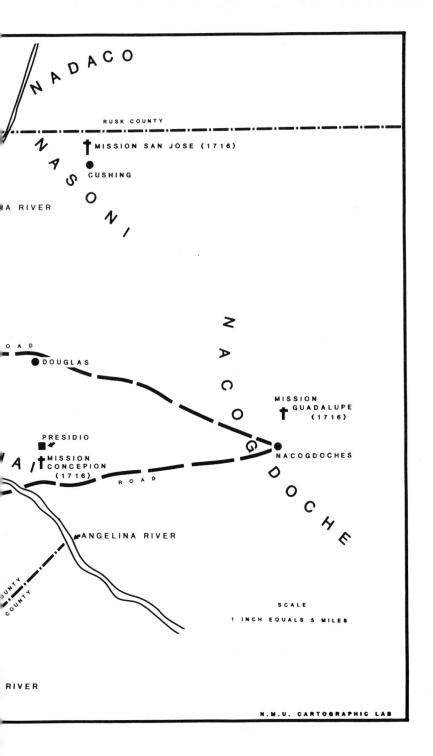

NADACO

NASONI

RUSK COUNTY

✝ MISSION SAN JOSE (1716)

● CUSHING

A RIVER

NACOGDOCHE

OAD

● DOUGLAS

MISSION
GUADALUPE
✝ (1716)

PRESIDIO
■↙

✝ MISSION
CONCEPION
(1716)

● NACOGDOCHES

ROAD

A

ANGELINA RIVER

UNTY
COUNTY

SCALE
1 INCH EQUALS 5 MILES

RIVER

N.M.U. CARTOGRAPHIC LAB

Angelina valleys. It is the early organization and society of this Neches-Angelina group that forms the theme of this book.

These southern Caddos are the tribes that have been commonly called the Texas, but more properly the Hasinais, or Asinais.[2] Their relatively advanced society gave them from the outset a proportionately large importance after the Europeans arrived, a fact that has not been duly emphasized. While it has been clearly shown that the immediate motive to planting the first Spanish establishments between the Red River and the Rio Grande was French encroachment, little note has been made of the previously acquired fame and the relative advancement of these Neches-Angelina tribes as factors in determining the Spanish choice of a location for a settlement.[3] Yet these were not unimportant considerations; indeed, they were primary. La Salle's colony, which first brought the Spaniards to Texas to colonize, was established on the Gulf coast; and had the natives of this region been as much talked of, as well organized, and as influential among the tribes, and therefore, as likely to become the theater of another French intrusion, the logical procedure would have been for the Spaniards to establish themselves on the ground where the French intrusion had occurred, especially as this was within relatively easy reach from Mexico by water and by land. But the cannibalistic Karankawan tribes of the coast proved hostile to French and Spaniards alike, and while on the one hand their savage life and inhospitable country offered little to attract the missionary, on the other hand their small

[2] A discussion of the meaning and application of the terms "Texas" and "Hasinai" forms a considerable portion of this paper and is presented in chap. 2.

[3] The authoritative presentation of the beginnings of the Spanish settlements in east Texas is that by Robert Carleton Clark, "The Beginnings of Texas," *Quarterly* of the Texas State Historical Association 5 (January, 1902): 171–205; and "Louis Juchereau de Saint-Denis and the Reestablishment of the Tejas Missions," *Quarterly* of the Texas State Historical Association 6 (July, 1902): 1–26. These excellent articles are marred to some extent by the author's failure to understand fully the organization of the Indian tribes and by the imperfect copies of some of his materials.

influence in the general native polity rendered them relatively useless as a basis for extending Spanish political authority.[4] These considerations entered prominently into the Spaniards' decision to establish their first Texas colony far in the interior, at a point difficult to reach from Mexico by land and wholly inaccessible by water.[5]

Events justified the Spanish estimate of the importance of the Neches-Angelina tribes as a base of political operations. But, although the control of the Hasinais and their Caddo neighbors remained for a century a cardinal point in the politics of the Texas-Louisiana frontier, it was soon learned that the weaker and more barbarous tribes of the San Antonio region, nearer Mexico and farther removed from the influence of the French, who soon followed the Spaniards into the Caddo country, afforded a better field for missionary labors.

Since native political organization was at best loose and shifting and was strongly dominated by ideas of independence, and since early writers were frequently indefinite in their use of terms, it would not be easy to determine with strict accuracy the constituent elements of this Neches-Angelina confederacy at different epochs.[6] However, a few of the leading tribes—those of greatest historical interest—stand out

[4]For studies of the Karankawan tribes see Albert S. Gatschet, "The Karankawa Indians," *Archaeological and Ethnological Papers of the Peabody Museum* 1 (1891): 21–103; Herbert E. Bolton, "The Founding of Mission Rosario: A Chapter in the History of the Gulf Coast," *Quarterly* of the Texas State Historical Association 10 (October, 1906): 113–39.

[5]These statements are not merely speculation but are based on positive evidence in the sources. The reports of the expedition of 1689 explicitly emphasize the superior civilization of the "Texas" as an argument for planting missions there. See letter of Alonso de León, May 18, 1689, in Buckingham Smith, ed., *Documentos para la historia de la Florida y tierra adyacentes*, 1: 25–28. See also Isidro Felix de Espinosa, *Chrónica apostólica, y seráphica de todos los colegios de propaganda fide de esta Nueva-España* pp. 408–409.

[6]The remainder of this chapter was published as Herbert E. Bolton, "The Native Tribes About the East Texas Missions," *Quarterly* of the Texas State Historical Association 11 (April, 1908): 249–76. This article is reprinted with the permission of the Texas State Historical Association.

with distinctness and can be followed for considerable periods of time.

Alonso De León learned in 1689 from the chief of the Nabedache tribe, the westernmost of the group, that his people had nine settlements.[7] Francisco de Jesús María Casañas, writing in 1691 near the Nabedache village after a fifteen months' residence there, reported that the "province of Aseney" comprised nine tribes, living in the Neches-Angelina valleys within a district about thirty-five leagues long. It would seem altogether probable that these two reports referred to the same nine tribes. Those named by Casañas, giving his different spellings, were the Nabadachos or Ynecis (Nabaydachos), Nechas (Neitas), Nechauis, Naconos, Nacachaus, Nazadachotzis, Cachaés (Catayes), Nabitis, and Nasayayas (Nasayahas).[8] The location of these tribes Casañas points out with some definiteness, and six of them, at least, we are able to identify in later times without question. Moreover, his description of their social organization is so minute that one concludes that he must have had accurate information. The testimony of a number of other witnesses who wrote between 1687 and 1692 in the main corroborates that of Casañas, particularly in the important matter of not including the Nasoni tribe within the Hasinai group.[9]

It so happens that after 1692 we get little intimate knowledge of the Hasinais until 1715. When light again dawns there appear in common usage one or two additions to Casañas's list. Whether they represent an oversight on his part or subse-

[7] Smith, ed., *Documentos*, pp. 25–28; see also Velasco, Dictamen Fiscal, November 30, 1716, Archivo General de Nación [hereafter AGN], Historia, vol. 2, fol. 179.

[8] Fray Francisco de Jesús María Casañas, Relación, August 15, 1691; AGN, Historia, vol. 394, fols. 7, 8, 12.

[9] Pierre Margry, ed. and trans., *Découvertes et établissements des français dans l'ouest et dans le sud de l'Amérique Septentrionale, 1614–1754*, 3: 341, 344ff. Benjamin F. French's version of Joutel's Journal, printed in *Historical Collections of Louisiana*, is very corrupt and must be used with the greatest care; Domingo Terán, "Derrotero," AGN, Historia, vol. 27, fols. 48ff.

quent accretions to the group we cannot certainly say. Of those in his list six, the Nabadachos, Neches, Nacogdoches, Nacachaus, Naconos, and Nabitis are mentioned under the same names by other writers. Cachaé is evidently Casañas's name for the well-known Hainais, as will appear later, while the Nabitis seem to be [Louis Juchereau] St. Denis's Nabiris and may be [Henri] Joutel's Noadiches (Nahordikes). For the Nechauis we can well afford to accept Casañas's explicit statement. Besides these nine, the Spaniards after 1716 always treated as within the Hasinai confederacy the Nasonis, Nadacos, and the Nacaos. Judging from the localities occupied and from some other circumstances, it is not altogether improbable that two of these may be old tribes under new names, as seems to be clearly the case with the Hainais. The Nasayaya, named by Casañas, may answer to the Nasonis, well known after 1716,[10] and the Nabitis may possibly be the Nadacos, also well known after that date. If both of these surmises be true, we must add to Casañas' list at least the Nacaos, making ten tribes in all; if not, there were at least eleven or twelve.

Putting first the best known and most important, they were: the Hainais, Nabedaches, Nacogdoches, Nasonis, Nadacos, Neches, Naconos, Nechauis, Nacaos, and perhaps, the Nabitis and the Nasayayas. This is not intended as a definitive list of the Hasinais at any one time, but it does include those known to have been within the compact area about the Querétaro missions and commonly treated as within the Hasinai

[10] The Nasayayas are placed by Casañas in a location corresponding very closely to that later occupied by the Nasonis. Yet that, though Casañas named the Nasonis he did not include them in the Hasinai group, while he did include the Nasayayas, and that Terán explicitly excludes the Nasonis from the Hasinais, make it seem probable that the Nasonis and the Nasayayas were distinct. The strongest ground for rejecting this conclusion is that the latter tribe never appears again under a recognizable name, unless they are the Nacaxes, who later appear on the Sabine River. The Nabitis might possibly be the Nadacos, but this does not seem likely, for the locations do not correspond very closely, while as late as 1715, St. Denis gave the Nabiris and Nadocos as two separate tribes.

group. By following the footnotes below it will be seen that "Nacoches," "Noaches," and "Asinay," which have been given, with resulting confusion, as names of tribes where early missions were established, are simply corruptions of "Neche," "Nasoni," and "Ainai," as the forms appear in the original manuscripts.

The Ais, or Eyeish, a neighbor tribe living beyond Arroyo Attoyac, at whose village a Zacatecan mission was founded in 1717, seem to have fallen outside the Hasinai confederacy. Only recently have they been included by ethnologists in the Caddoan stock, and, although they are now regarded as Caddoans, there are indications that their dialect was quite different from that of their western neighbors, while their manners and customs were always regarded as inferior to those of these other tribes.[11] Moreover, there is some evidence that they were generally regarded as aliens, and that they were sometimes even positively hostile to the Hasinais. Thus, Casañas includes them in his list of the enemies of the Hasinais; Espinosa, a quarter of a century after Casañas wrote, speaks of them as friendly toward the "Assinay," from which by implication he excludes them, but says that the Hasinai medicine men "make all the tribes believe that disease originates in the bewitchment that the neighboring Indians, the Bidais, Ays, and Yacdocas, cause them," a belief that clearly implies hostility between the tribes concerned, while Mézières wrote in 1779 that the Ais were hated alike by their Spanish and their Indian neighbors.[12]

The Adaes, in whose midst the mission of Nuestra Señora de los Dolores was founded in 1717, lived beyond the Sabine River and belonged to the Red River group of Caddoans, that is, to the Caddos. They therefore do not fall within the scope of this work.

[11] On the subject of their language see Hodge, ed., *Handbook* 1: 448–49.
[12] Espinosa, *Chrónica*, p. 428; Athanase de Mézières to Teodoro de Croix, May 27, 1779, AGN, Historia, vol. 28, fol. 240.

Their Locations

For determining the location of these tribes our chief materials are the Journal of Joutel (1687), the Relación of Francisco de Jesús María Casañas (1691), De León's diary of the expedition of 1690, [Domingo de] Terán's for that of 1691–92, those of [Domingo] Ramón and [Isidro Felix de] Espinosa for the expedition of 1716, [Juan de la] Peña's for that of Aguayo (1721), [Pedro de] Rivera's for his *visita* of 1727, [Fray Gaspár José de] Solís's for that made by him in 1767–68, and [Athanase] Mézières's account of his tours among the Indians in 1772, 1778, and 1779.[13] Besides these and numerous supplementing documentary sources, there are (1) the early surveys showing the Camino Real, or Old San Antonio Road, whose windings in eastern Texas were determined mainly by the location of the principal Indian villages where the Spaniards had settlements, (2) certain unmistakable topographical features, such as the principal rivers and the Neches Indian mounds, and (3) geographical names that have come down to us from the period of Spanish occupation.

It will be interesting, before studying the location of each one of the tribes separately, to read the general description of the group given by Casañas in 1691. Speaking of the official called the Great Chenesi, he said:

[13] Of the diaries of De León and Espinosa, I cite only the manuscripts in the AGN. These, I believe, are not otherwise available and have not before been used except by R. C. Clark, who has recently [1907] had access to my transcripts. Of Casañas's Relación I follow an autograph manuscript, which, however, appears to be a copy instead of the original. Of the diaries of Terán and Ramón I have had access to the originals, and of the Mézières manuscripts either to the originals or to certified official copies. My copy of the Rivera diary is from the edition printed in 1736. For the Peña and Solís diaries I have had to depend on the copies in the Historia. On comparing Historia transcripts, in general, with the originals, I have found that they are very corrupt and that numerous mistakes have resulted from their use. However, in cases where there are no essential differences, I cite the Historia copies, because they are more generally accessible; otherwise I cite the originals.

To him are subject all of these nine tribes: The Nabadacho, which for another name, is called Yneci. Within this tribe are founded the mission of Nuestro Padre San Francisco and the one I have founded in Your Excellency's name [viceroy conde de Galve], that of El Santíssimo Nombre de María. The second tribe is that of the Necha. It is separated from the former by the Rio el Arcángel San Miguel [the Neches]. Both are between north and east.[14] At one side of these two, looking south, between south and east, is the tribe of Nechaui, and half a league from the last, another called the Nacono. Toward the north, where the above-mentioned Necha tribe ends, is the tribe called Nacachau. Between this tribe and another called Nazadachotzi, which is toward the east, in the direction of the house of the Great Chenesi, which is about . . . half way between these two tribes, comes another. It begins at the house of the Great Chenesi, between north and east, and is called Cachaé. At the end of this tribe, looking toward the north, is another called Nabiti, and east of this another called Nasayaha. These nine tribes embrace an extent of about thirty-five leagues and all are subject to this Great Chenesi.[15]

This description will be convenient for reference as we proceed.

It may be noted here that the leagues [one league is about two miles] of the old Spanish diaries of expeditions into Texas are not air-line distances but include the many crooks and turns of the trails. One should keep this in mind when reading the data hereafter presented.

The Nacogdoche Tribe and the Mission of Guadalupe

A starting point or base from which to determine the location of most of the tribes is the founding of the mission of Nuestra Señora de Guadalupe at the main village of Nacogdoches in 1716, for it can be shown that this mission remained on the same site until it was abandoned in 1773; that the modern city of Nacogdoches was built at the old mission site; and, there-

[14]Editor's note: Meaning north and east of the point where Bolton is writing, near San Pedro Creek, Houston County, as appears below.

[15]Casañas, Relación, fols. 7–8.

fore, that the location of this city represents the location of the principal Nacogdoche village.

The evidence briefly stated is as follows: Ramón, whose expedition founded this mission, wrote in his "Derrotero" that nine leagues east-southeast of the principal Hasinai village (the Hainais), on the Angelina River, he arrived at the "village of the Nacogdoches," and that on the next day he "set out from this mission," implying clearly that the mission was located where he had been writing, at the Nacogdoche village.[16] As is well known, all the missions of this section were abandoned in 1719 because of fear of a French invasion. Peña reports in his diary of the [Marqués de] Aguayo expedition of 1721 that Aguayo, who restored the abandoned missions, entered "the place where stood the mission of N. S. de Guadalupe de Nacodoches," and rebuilt the church. The inference is that the site was the old one, more especially since in one instance in the same connection where a mission site was changed Peña mentions the fact.[17] This mission was continued without any known change until 1773, when it was abandoned. But when in 1779 (not 1778, as is sometimes stated) Antonio Gil Ybarbo laid the foundations of modern Nacogdoches with his band of refugees from the Trinity River settlement of Bucareli, he found the Nacogdoches mission buildings still standing, settled his colony near them, and apparently reoccupied some of them.[18]

Hence it is clear that the city of Nacogdoches represents very closely, perhaps exactly, the site of the main village of the Nacogdoche tribe at the end of the seventeenth century. If more evidence were necessary, the presence within the city of

[16] Domingo Ramón, "Derrotero," pp. 135–59. The copy in Historia is very corrupt. At this point a generous addition is made by the copiest. See folio 158.

[17] Juan de la Peña, Diario, AGN, Historia, vol. 28, fols. 40, 43, 44.

[18] Antonio Gil Ybarbo to Teodoro de Croix, May 13, 1779, in "Expediente sobre el abandano del pueblo de Nuestra Señora del Pilar de Bucareli (1778–1780), AGN, Historia, vol. 51, fols. 21–23; See Herbert E. Bolton, "The Old Stone Fort at Nacogdoches," *Quarterly* of the Texas State Historical Association 9 (October, 1905): 283–85.

Nacogdoches until recent times of four ancient Indian mounds would strengthen the conclusion.[19] With this as a starting point it is not difficult to indicate the approximate location of the most prominent of the remaining tribes. Beginning with the Nacogdoches involves the disadvantage of reading the diaries backwards, it is true—for they generally record an eastward journey—but it has the great advantage of enabling us to proceed from a well-established point.

The Hainai Tribe and the Mission of La Concepción

On the east bank of the Angelina River, a little north of a direct west line from the Nacogdoche village, was that of the Hainais.[20] This tribe, whose lands lay on both sides of the Angelina, was the head of the Hasinai confederacy and for that reason was sometimes called Hasinais.[21] It is to this village, also, that the name Texas was usually applied when it was restricted to a single tribe. Within its territory was the chief temple of the group, presided over by the Great Chenesi, or high priest,[22] and at its main village the mission of La Purísima Concepción was founded in 1716.

[19] Information was furnished in 1907 by Dr. J. E. Mayfield, of Nacogdoches, who writes: "Four similar mounds once existed at Nacogdoches, located upon a beautiful site about three hundred yards north-east of the old stone fort or stone house that has recently been removed from the main city plaza. . . . These have been razed and almost obliterated. To the east of them is a hole or excavation from which the earth may have been taken for the construction of these mounds." Editor's note: This letter was not found in the Bolton Papers. On August 31, 1971, only one mound remained in Nacogdoches, at 519 North Mound Street. Artifacts from a larger mound are housed in the Old Stone Fort Museum, on the Stephen F. Austin State University campus.

[20] I follow the spelling of James Mooney, which has been adopted by the Bureau of American Ethnology. The more common Spanish forms were Aynay and Ainai. English writers frequently spell it Ioni.

[21] Espinosa, Chrónica, p. 425; Ramón, "Derrotero," fol. 153; Mézières to Croix, August 26, 1779, AGN, Historia, vol. 28, fol. 241.

[22] Casañas, Relación, fols. 10, 15, 36; Espinosa, Chrónica, p. 423.

After the Relación of Casañas, our next sources of specific information on the location of this village are the diaries. Ramón tells us that he entered the "Pueblo de los Ainai" just east of the Angelina River and that nine leagues east-southeast of this village he reached the "Pueblo de los Nacogdoches."[23] The missionary fathers who accompanied Ramón, in their Representación made at the same time, reported the distance as eight leagues east-southeast. Peña (1721) says the distance was eight leagues east-northeast from the presidio founded near the mission and nine from the mission. Rivera (1727) found the mission just east of the "Río de los Aynays," or the Angelina, and nine leagues west of the Nacogdoches mission.[24] These witnesses tally in the main with each other and also, be it noted, with the testimony of the San Antonio Road, as its route is identified in the old surveys. According to the best information obtainable it ran from Nacogdoches a little north of west to the Angelina, passing it about at Linwood Crossing.[25] Espinosa tells us that he founded the mission of [La] Conceptión a mile or two east of the place where the

[23] Ramón, "Derrotero," entries for July 7 and 8. The original is in the AGN. The copy in Historia, vol. 28, fols. 157–58, changes "Ainai" to "Asinay" and "Nacogdoches" to "Nacodoches." It is evidently such errors as the former that gave rise to the idea that there was an Asinay tribe. Similarly, the Historia copy of the Representación of the Padres Misioneros dated July 22, 1716, AGN, Historia, vol. 28, fol. 163, states that the mission of Concepción was founded for the "Asinays," whereas the original of that document, as of Espinosa's diary, reads "Ainai." This error has been copied and popularized.

[24] Ramón, "Derrotero," fol. 158; Padres Misioneros, Representación, fol. 153; Peña, Diario, fols. 43–44; Pedro de Rivera y Villalón, Diario y Derrotero de lo caminado, visita, y obcervado en el discurso de la visita general de Precidios, situados en las Provincias Internas de Nueva España, leg. 2140.

[25] Maps of Cherokee and Nacogdoches counties (1879) by I. C. Walsh, commissioner of the General Land Office of Texas, compiled from official data. Editor's note: In a letter dated October 5, 1971, David A. Reeves, director of records of the General Land Office of Texas, stated that these maps could not be located.

highway crosses the Angelina, near two springs, in the middle of the Hainai village. This site could not have been far from Linwood Crossing.[26]

This Hainai tribe, as has been stated, was evidently the one which Casañas called the Cachaés or Catayes. He said that between the Nacachaus and the Nacogdoches, about midway, was the lodge of the Great Chenesi, and—if we get his meaning here—that immediately northeast of this lodge was the Cachaé tribe. From other data we learn that the Chenesi's house was within or on the borders of the Hainai territory, about three leagues from the mission of La Concepción and apparently west of the Angelina River.[27] The Cachaés thus correspond, in location and relations, to the Hainais, while, moreover, the latter are the only tribe that appear in this locality after 1716. Considering with these facts the probability that Casañas would hardly have left the head tribe unmentioned in so formal a description as is his, and the fact that the Hainais are clearly the head tribe, it seems reasonably certain that the Cachaés and Hainais were identical.

The Neche Tribe and the Mission of San Francisco (Second Site)

Southwest of the Hainai village, nearly straight west of the Nacogdoches, was the Neche village, near the east bank of the Neches River and near the crossing of the Camino Real. The diaries usually represent the distance from the Neches to the Hainais as about the same as that from the Hainais to the Nacogdoches—some eight or nine leagues.[28] The air-line distance was evidently somewhat less in the former case than in

[26] Isidro Felix de Espinosa, Diario, July 6 and 7, 1716, AGN, Historia, vol. 394, fols. 130–31; Ramón, "Derrotero," fol. 158.

[27] Espinosa, Chrónica, p. 424.

[28] Espinosa tells us that the mission was near a spring and also near an arroyo that flowed from the northeast. He gave the distance from the mission to the camp near the Neches River as one league and that to the mission of Concepción, east of the Angelina, eight leagues, going northeast

the latter, but the route was less direct, since between the Neches and the Angelina rivers the road swings quite decidedly to the north. The usual crossing of the Neches, by this highway as now identified, was at Williams' Ferry, below the mouth of San Pedro Creek.[29]

Archaeological remains help us to identify this ford and give certainty to the approximate correctness of our conclusions. These remains are the Indian mounds east of the Neches River. The first mention of them that I have seen is that by Mézières in 1779. His record is important. Passing along the Camino Real on his way to Nabedache, he noted the large mound near the Neches River, raised, he said, by the ancestors of the natives of the locality "in order to build on its summit a temple, which overlooked the pueblo near by, and in which they worshipped their gods—a monument rather to their great numbers than to the industry of their individuals."[30] This mound and its two less conspicuous companions still stand in Cherokee County about a mile and a half from the river and five miles southwest of Alto, in a plain known to some as Mound Prairie, undoubtedly the true Mound Prairie whose whereabouts has been debated. They are on land now the property of the Merrill Orchard Company, once a part of the original grant made to the romantic Pedro Ellis Bean. The Old San Antonio Road, as identified in the oldest surveys, ran about three hundred yards north of the largest mound, which

by east, then east: Espinosa, Diario, July 2 and 6, 1716, fols. 129–30. Ramón gave the distance to the mission of Concepción, apparently from the camp near the Neches but possibly from the mission, as nine leagues east-northeast: Ramón, "Derrotero," fols. 157–58.

[29] See maps cited above and also map of Houston County, copied from a map by George Aldrich by H. S. Upshur, draftsman in the General Land Office, 1841. Editor's note: See reference in note 25 above.

[30] Mézières to Croix, August 26, 1779, in AGN. This letter was written at the "Village of Sn. Pedro de los Navedachos" just after Mézières passed the mounds. The Historia copy of the letter gives the name of the place, erroneously, as San Pedro Nevadachos; see vol. 28, fol. 241.

is also the northernmost.[31] This mound, standing by the old highway, is an important western landmark for the location of the early tribes and missions, just as the site of Nacogdoches is an important eastern landmark. With the evidence of these mounds, the name San Pedro attached to the creek joining the Neches just above the crossing, and the early maps of the Camino Real, there is no doubt as to the approximate location of the old crossing and, consequently, of their respective missions, on opposite sides of the river.[32]

The mission of San Francisco de los Texas, reestablished in 1716 at the Neche village,[33] appears from the diaries to have been one or two leagues from the crossing. Peña's diary puts it at two leagues. The entry in his diary for August 3, 1721, is as follows: "The bridge [over the Neches] having been completed, all the people, the equipage, and the drove, crossed in good order, taking the direction of east-northeast, and camp was made near the mission of San Francisco, where the presidio was placed the second time it was moved in 1716. The march was only two leagues."[34] Rivera gives the distance from the crossing as more than a league.[35] The other diaries are

[31] Editor's note: These mounds are now on the property of the Indian Mound Nursery of the Texas State Forest Service. The largest of the mounds was marked in 1936 and 1969.

[32] Information furnished by Dr. J. E. Mayfield, of Nacogdoches. The original Austin map (1829) in the Secretaría de Fomento, Mexico, shows the mound on the north side of the road.

[33] On the authority of the corrupt copy of Ramón's itinerary in Historia, vol. 28, fol. 157, it has been stated that this mission was founded at the "Nacoches" village, a tribal name nowhere else encountered. The original of the itinerary, however, gives the name Naiches, thus agreeing with the other original reports and clearing up a troublesome uncertainty. The official name of the mission was San Francisco de los Texas, but, because of its location at the Neche village it came to be called, popularly, San Francisco de los Neches.

[34] Terán, "Derrotero," fol. 38. The presidio had been temporarily placed in 1716 on the west side of the Neches, near a small lake, and then moved across the river.

[35] Rivera, Diario, leg. 2140.

indefinite on this point, but the conclusion is plain that the mission and the Neches village were close to the mounds, the mission, at least, being apparently farther from the river.

The Nabedache Tribe and the Mission of San Francisco
(First Site)

The westernmost tribe of the group was the Nabedache. The main village was a short distance—perhaps six miles—west of the Neches River, above the crossing, near a stream that early became known as San Pedro, and at a site that took the name San Pedro de los Nabedachos. It is the name San Pedro that has caused some persons to think, groundlessly, that the first mission of San Francisco was founded at San Antonio, because of the presence there of San Pedro Springs.

The exact point at which the main Nabedache village stood I cannot say, but certain data enables us to approximate its location pretty closely. First is the testimony of the diaries and other early documents. De León reported in his itinerary (1690) that from the camp half a league from the Nabedache chief's house to the Neches River, going northeast, it was three leagues.[36] The site examined on the river at this point was deemed unsuitable for the mission "because it was so far out of the way of the Indians"; consequently the mission was established close to the camp "in the middle" of the village. In their reports to the home government [Damián] Massanet and De León seem to have stated that the mission was some two leagues from the Neches;[37] while Terán in 1691 reported it to be only a league and a half from the Mission of Santísimo Nombre de María, which was evidently close to the Neches

[36] De Leon, "Derrotero," entry for May 26, 1691. He recorded the distance going and coming as six leagues.

[37] Ibid., entry for May 27; Fray Damian Massanet, "Carta de Don Damian Mazanet a Don Carlos de Siguenza y Góngora Sobre el Descubrimiento de la Bahia de Espiritu Santo," trans. Lilia M. Casis, Quarterly of the Texas State Historical Association 2 (April, 1899): 253–312.

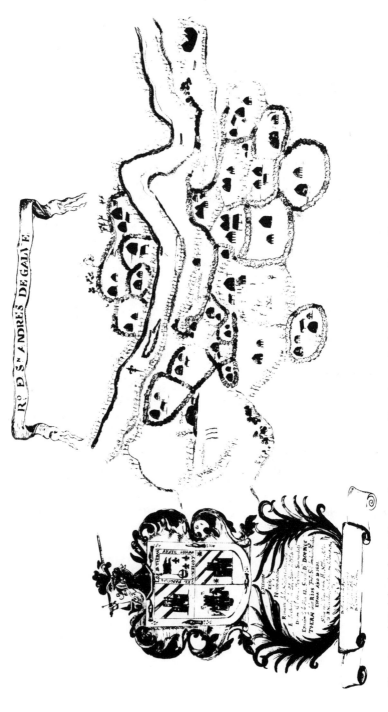

Drawing of Kadohadacho Indian settlements near Texarkana similar to those of the Hasinai. Seen here are various private and public structures and boats in the stream. Based on Terán's *to drawing of San Cruz*

River.[38] Casañas and Espinosa said that the village was about three leagues from this river, the former adding that it was right across the stream from the Neche tribe.[39] Joutel and Ramón called the distance from center to center of the two villages about five leagues.[40] In comparing these estimates with those that follow we must remember that it was somewhat farther from the village to the crossing of the river than to the river at its nearest point, for as early as 1691 it was found that the best crossing was downstream a league or more.[41]

Keeping these things in mind, it may be noted that Peña's diary makes the distance from San Pedro to the crossing four leagues. In his entry for July 27, 1721, he says, "The Father President F. Ysidro Felix de Espinosa went ahead with the chief of the Texas, who wished to go to arrange beforehand the reception in *the place where the first mission had been.*" In his entry for the next day he says, "Following the same direction of east-northeast, the journey was continued to the place of S. Pedro . . . *where the presidio and mission had been placed, for the Spaniards did not go beyond this point in the year '90.*" Here the reception was held, and presents were given to Aguayo by the Indians of the "ranchos which are near by," the point being, according to Peña's diary, fifteen leagues northeast from the crossing of the Trinity,[42] and four from the cross-

[38] This is an inference from the instructions given in 1691 to Terán and Gregorio Salinas, which required them to examine the large stream two leagues, more or less, from the village where the mission of San Francisco had been established the year before. See Terán, "Ynstrucciones dadas. . . ," January 23, 1691, AGN, Historia, vol. 27, fol. 19; Gregorio Salinas, "Ynstrucción que han de observar el Capp. D. Gregorio Salinas. . . ," April 13, 1691, AGN, Provincias Internas, vol. 182, fols. 445–48. This document has not been used before.

[39] Casañas, Relación, fols. 2, 6.

[40] Margry, ed. and trans., *Decouvertes*, 3: 341–44; Ramón, "Derrotero," fol. 157.

[41] Terán, "Dérrotero," fol. 47, 61.

[42] Peña, Diario, fol. 34–35. The italics are mine. It may be noted that Peña and Rivera give quite commonly shorter leagues than the other.

Archaeologists excavating a Hasinai site on the ground of the Indian Mound Nursery of the Texas State Forest Service, five miles southwest of Alto, Texas, in the 1930s. Courtesy Texas Archaeological Research Lab, University of Texas, Austin.

ing of the Neches, passing by the site of the presidio as it was first established in 1716.

Rivera's diary makes the distance from San Pedro to the crossing something over four leagues, or six to the mission on the other side. His record is interesting. He writes, on August 5, "I camped this day near a prairie which they call San Pedro de los Nabidachos, formerly occupied by Indians of the tribe of this name, but at present by the Neches tribe, of the group of the Aynays, head tribe of the Province of Texas." His next entry begins, "This day, the sixth, . . . continuing the march in the same direction [east-one-fourth-northeast] I traveled six leagues, crossing the Río de los Neches. At more than a league's distance from it I found some huts where a religious of the Cross of Querétaro resides, appointed . . . to minister to these Indians . . . with the name of San Francisco de Neches," that is, the mission having this name.[43] Solís, going northeast in 1767, tells us that San Pedro de los Nabedachos was beyond the San Pedro River. He may possibly have meant that it was on the north side, but I am inclined to think that he meant that it was east of one of the southern branches.[44]

Our inference from the diaries would thus be that the first site of the mission of San Francisco, in the village of the Nabedache, was from one and a half to three leagues—from three to eight miles—distant from the Neches River at its nearest point, a league or more farther from the crossing, and still another league—in all perhaps ten miles—from the Neches village on the other side of the river.

The information of the diaries is here supplemented by geo-

[43] Brackets are Bolton's. Rivera, *Diario*, leg. 2140. Ramón's "Derrotero" makes the distance four leagues from San Pedro to his camp near the Neches or to the mission site across the river, but it is not clear which, although the former is probably his meaning; Ramón, "Derrotero," fols. 155–57. Ramón's Representación makes the distance between the first mission of San Francisco, and the second of this name, at the Neche village, five leagues. Ibid., fol. 159.

[44] "Expedition of Mézières," March 9, 1778, AGN, Historia, vol. 28, fol. 279.

graphical names. San Pedro Creek, which joins the Neches River in the northern part of Houston County, still bears the name that was early given to the vicinity of the Nabedache village and the first mission of San Francisco. Apparently this occurred in 1716 when Espinosa and Ramón celebrated the feast of San Pedro there. The ceremony took place at a spot which, according to both Ramón and Espinosa, was thirteen leagues northeast of the crossing of the Trinity.[45] That the name was continuously applied to the place until after the middle of the eighteenth century is sufficiently established by the citations already made. Of its continued use subsequently there is an abundance of evidence.[46]

Next comes the testimony of the Camino Real, or the Old San Antonio Road. There seems to be no good topographical reason why this old highway should not have run directly from Crockett to the Neches at Williams's Ferry, and the long curve to the north between these points must be explained as a detour to the Nabedache village and the missions located nearby. The surveys represent this highway as running always south of San Pedro Creek, never crossing it, but definitely directed toward it at a point some six or eight miles west of the Neches crossing. The point corresponds closely to that designated in the diaries. Near here, quite certainly, were the Nabedache village and the first mission of San Francisco, while not far away, but nearer the Neches River, was the second mission

[45] Ramón, Representación, July 22, 1716, AGN, Historia, vol. 27, fol. 159. Ramón, "Derrotero," and Espinosa, Diario, entries for June 29–30.

[46] Ramón, "Derrotero," and Espinosa, Diario (1716), entries for June 29–30; Peña, Diario (1721), fol. 34; Rivera, Diario, leg. 2140; Fray Gaspar José de Solís, Diario, AGN, Historia, vol. 27, fol. 279; "Expedition of Mézières," AGN, Historia, vol. 28, fol. 270; Cristóbal de Córdoba to Manuel de Munòz, Nacogdoches, December 3, 1793, Bexar Archives, roll 24, frames 0098–99. It may be noted that although the post office village of San Pedro preserves the name of the general locality, it is too far west to answer to the site of the mission of San Francisco and the Nabedache village.

established in that region, that of El Santísimo Nombre de María, founded in the autumn of 1690.[47]

The Nacachau, Nechaui, and Nacono Tribes

Across the Neches River from the Nabedache village, only a few leagues away and adjoining the Neche tribe on the north, was the relatively little known tribe called by Casañas the Nacachaus and by Hildalgo the Nacachaos. We have seen that Casañas described the Neche tribe as being separated from the Nabedaches only by the Neches River. Later he says, "Toward the north, where the above-mentioned Neche tribe ends, is that called the Nacachaus." The Neche and Nacachau villages were thus close together. Near them the second mission of San Francisco was founded in 1716. Ramón says that the mission was founded in the village of the Naiches, and the missionary fathers say that it was for the "Naicha, Nabeitdâche, Nocono, and Nacâchao" villages.[48]

Southeast of the Neche and the Nabedache villages, according to Casañas, were two villages half a league apart,

[47] This mission was close to or on the bank of the Neches River. According to Terán's itinerary (1691) it was a league upstream from the crossing and a league and a half northeast of the mission of San Francisco. See Terán, "Descripción," fols. 45, 47, 61; Casañas, Relación, fol. 104, said that it was on the bank of the river.

[48] Casañas, Relación, fols. 107–108; Ramón, "Derrotero," fol. 158; Padres Missioneros, Representación, fol. 163; Peña, Diario, fols. 38–41; Rivera, Diario, leg. 2140; Antonio Bonilla, "Bonilla's Brief Compendium of the History of Texas, 1772," trans. Elizabeth H. West, Quarterly of the Texas State Historical Association 8 (July, 1904): 35, 38. As I have indicated above, the Historia copy of Ramón's itinerary states that the mission was founded in the village of the "Nacoches," a miscopy for "Naiches." The map on page [?] was made before I discovered this error in the copy, which I had first used. My opinion now is that, with the correction, the sources would not be violated by placing the Nacachua tribe somewhat farther north than I have there represented it. Editor's note: The map discussed here has not been located.

called the Nechauis and the Naconos. Of the Nechauis we do not hear again, but from Peña (1721) we learn that the Nacono village, which he called El Macono, was five leagues below the Neches crossing. This would put the Nechaui and the Nacono villages five leagues down the Neches River, perhaps one on each side.[49]

The Nasoni Tribe and the Mission of San José

Above the Hainais, on the waters of the Angelina, were the Nasonis. Joutel in 1687 reached their village after going from the Nabedache twelve leagues eastward, plus an unestimated distance north. Terán in 1691 found it twelve leagues northeast of the Neches crossing below the Nabedache village.[50] The founding in 1716 of a mission for this tribe and the Nadaco gives us more definite data for its location. The missionaries who took part in the expedition, in their joint report called the distance from the Hainais to the Nacogdoches eight leagues east-southeast, and that from the Hainais to the Nasoni mission seven northeast. Peña, who called the former distance nine leagues east-northeast, estimated the latter as eight north. Espinosa put it at seven northeast.[51] Thirty years later Espinosa said that the mission was founded in the Nasoni tribe and ten leagues from the mission of La Concepción.[52] This increase in his estimate of the distance may be due to his long absence from the country.

[49] Casañas, Relación, fol. 108; Peña, Diario, fol. 36. As the Nacono visited Aguayo on the west side of the Neches, I have represented the village on that side in my map. Of course, the reason is very slight. Espinosa in his diary says that the Nasoni mission was founded for the Naconos, but this seems to be a form of Nasoni, for by others it is uniformly called the mission of the Nasonis or of the Nadacos, or of both.

[50] Margry, ed. and trans., Découvertes, 3: 337–40; Terán, "Derrotero," fols. 47–48.

[51] Padres Missioneros, Representación, fol. 163; Peña, Diario, fol. 44; Espinosa, Diario (1716), fol. 131.

[52] Espinosa, Chrónica, p. 418.

The direction of the Nasoni mission from that of La Concepción, therefore, was evidently northeast, and the distance about the same, perhaps a trifle less, than that to the Nacogdoche village.

Espinosa, who in 1716 went over the route from the Hainais to the Nasonis to establish the mission of San José, recorded in his diary that on the way there were many Indian houses (*ranchos*), and that the mission was situated "on an arroyo with plentiful water running north." We must look, therefore, for a point some fifteen or more miles northeast of the Hainais on a stream running northward. These conditions would be satisfied only by one of the southern tributaries of Shawnee Creek, near the north line of Nacogdoches County. In this vicinity, clearly, was the Nasoni settlement in 1716. It seems not to have changed its location essentially since it had been visited by Joutel and Terán a quarter of a century before, and it remained in the same vicinity another third of a century, for in 1752, [Manuel Antonio] de Soto Bermúdez found the Nasoni village eleven leagues northward from the Nacogdoches mission.[53] The mission of San José remained near the Nasonis until 1729, when, like those of San Francisco, at the Neches village, and [La] Concepción, at the Hainai village, it was removed to San Antonio.

The Nadaco

For the rest of the tribes in this group our information is less definite. The Nadaco, though a prominent tribe, cannot be located with certainty until 1787, when they, or at least a part of them, were on the Sabine River, apparently in the northern part of Panolo County.[54] But in 1716 they were clearly

[53] Manuel Antonio de Soto Bermudez, Investigación, November 12, 1752. AGN, Provincias Internas, vol. 181, fol. 134.

[54] Francisco Xavier Fragoso, Diario, 1788, in the General Land Office, Austin, Texas, Records, vol. 68, p. 174, and also in AGN, Historia, vol. 143, fols. 1–14.

near the Nasonis, and sometimes the two tribes seem to have
been considered as one. Hildalgo, who must have known, for
he was on the ground, distinctly states that the mission of San
José was founded for the Nasonis and the Nadacos.[55] Although
the mission was commonly known to the Spaniards as that of
the Nasonis, the French writers in particular, including St.
Denis, sometimes called it the Nadaco mission.[56] Frequent ref-
erences made by [Bénard] La Harpe in 1719 to the Nadacos
show that he is speaking either of the Nasonis or of a tribe
in their immediate vicinity, more probably the latter, since in
other instances the tribes are so clearly distinguished. For instance, he tells us that when he was at the Kadohadacho village on the Red River, not far from the site of Texarkana,
"they assured me that sixty leagues south was the village of the
Nadacos, where the Spaniards had a mission, and that they

[55] The Historia copy of Ramón's itinerary ("Derrotero," fol. 158) calls this
mission that of the "Noachis," but the original reads plainly "Nasonis."

[56] Thus La Harpe noted in his journal that St. Denis, who conducted the
expedition of 1716 that founded the missions "proposed, sometime after his
arrival, that he should be the conductor of nine missionaries to the tribes of
the Adayes, Ayches, Nacocodochys, Inays and Nadacos" in "Extrait du
Journal manuscrit du voyage de la Louis de l'Ouest de cette colonie," in
Margry, ed. and trans., Decouvertes, 4: 194. St. Denis himself regarded the
mission as having been founded in the Nadaco tribe. This is the inference
from a correspondence carried on in 1735–36 between him and Manuel de
Sandoval, governor of Texas. Sandoval wrote to St. Denis on March 10,
1736, acknowledging a letter of December 2, 1735, in which St. Denis
outlined the basis of French claims to country west of the Red River. To
judge from Sandoval's summary of the letter (I have not seen the letter), he
alleged that, with Bienville, he had explored the country as far back as
1702; that in 1715 he had journeyed from the "Asinais" to Mexico, seeing
on the way only vestiges of the old Spanish settlements; that he conducted
Ramón into the country, "the result of which was the foundation [of mis-
sions], which it was requested of your lordship should be established among
the Nacodoches, Nadacos, Ainais, and Naichas, and the subsequent ones
among the Ays and Adais, maintaining the ministers of the Gospel at your
expense." Manuel de Sandoval to St. Denis, March 10, 1736, AGN, Historia, vol. 524, fols. 107–11. With this letter there are several original letters
of St. Denis.

had another among the Assinais, in the Amediche [Nabe-
dache] tribe, which was seventy leagues south-by-southwest
from the Nassonites [which were near the Kadohadacho]."[57]
In 1752 the Nadacos were only a short distance northward
from the Nasonis, apparently northeast, and the two tribes
then had a single chief.[58]

Supposing the Nadacos and the Nasonis to have lived in
clearly distinct settlements at the early period, the Nadacos
could hardly have been near the highway from the Nasonis to
the Kadohadachos, for, as we have seen, the Nasonis always
figure as the last station on the way to the Kadohadachos. It
seems more probable, considering this last fact together with
the statements made about the mission of San José, that the
two tribes lived in a settlement practically continuous, to
which sometimes one and sometimes the other name was
given. An upper branch of the Angelina is now called Ana-
darko (Nadaco) Creek, and it is possible, in spite of the above
considerations, that this stream was the home of the Nadacos
at the coming of the Spaniards and the French, but it seems
more probable that it was applied in later times as a result of
the removal of the tribe to that neighborhood.

It is clear, at any rate, that in the early eighteenth century
the Nadaco village was very near that of the Nasonis.

Other Tribes

Of the location of remaining tribes we know even less than of
the Nadacos and can only record the few statements made of
them by the early writers. Three leagues west of the Nasonis,
Joutel entered the village of the Noadiches (Nahordikes)[59]
who, he said, were allies of the Cenis [Asinais] and had the

---

[57] Margry, ed and trans., *Découvertes*, 6: 262.
[58] This is on the well-founded assumption that the Nadotes discussed by
De Soto Bermudez were the same as the Nadacos; Bermudez, Investigación,
fol. 135.
[59] Margry, ed. and trans., *Découvertes*, 3: 388.

same customs. This location corresponds with that assigned by Casañas to the Nabitis, and the tribes may have been identical. The site designated was apparently west of the Angelina River and near the southwestern corner of Rusk County. Similarly, the Nasayayas, put by Casañas east of the Nabitis, may possibly have been the Nasonis. If they were a separate tribe, they must have been in the same neighborhood. If separate, too, they early disappear from notice, unless possibly they may be the Nacaxes, who later are found in the same latitude, but farther east. All that we can say of the location of the Nacoas is that they were northward from the Nacogdoches and probably closer to the Nacogdoches than to the Nasonis, since they were attached to the Nacogdoche mission. A reasonable conjecture is that they were in the neighborhood of the Nacaniche Creek, in Nacogdoches County.[60]

Thus, with varying degrees of precision and confidence, we are able from a study of the documents to indicate the early homes of the tribes usually included in the Hasinai group. Five of the sites, at least, are quite definitely established, and these are historically the most important, for they were the sites of Spanish establishments, while the others were not. I refer, of course, to the villages of the Nabedaches, Neches, Hainais, Nacogdoches, and Nasonis. A careful examination of the topography of the country and of the archaeological remains will doubtless enable one to verify some and to modify others of the conclusions here set forth.

[60] Casañas puts the Nacogdoche tribe east and the Nacau tribe northeast of his mission. He says in another passage that the Nacaos constituted a province distinct from the Aseneys and thirty leagues from the Nabedaches.

2

The Names Texas and Hasinai

Since this group of tribes has been called both Texas and Hasinai, without a clear understanding of the applicability of either name and with a good deal of confusion, the meaning and application of both terms demand a fuller discussion than they have heretofore received.[1]

The name Texas has been variously applied by writers, but by the Spaniards, from whom the French and the English borrowed it—a fact not to be forgotten—it was most commonly used to designate the tribes of the Neches-Angelina valley, the people under consideration here. In Spanish writings there are many deviations from this usage, it is true, but this is the popular one. As a geographical term the name was first applied to the immediate country of these Neches-Angelina tribes, and then was gradually extended to all the territory included within the present state of Texas; that is to say, the name Texas, like the boundaries of the province, with empire wended its way westward.

Just when and how the name Texas first reached the Span-

[1] On the authority of James Mooney, who has lived among the survivors of these tribes and whose testimony on this point should be trustworthy, I have adopted the spelling Hasinai instead of the more usual Spanish forms "Asinai" and "Asinay." See James Mooney, *The Ghost-Dance Religion*, Fourteenth Annual Report of the Bureau of American Ethnology (1896), p. 1092. Nevertheless, this spelling is historically not as well authenticated as Asinai.

iards is unknown and will probably always remain a mystery. But it is certain that in the seventeenth century there was current in New Spain the notion of a "great kingdom of Texas," parallel with and even associated with the notion of a "Gran Quivira." Passing by earlier notices,[2] the idea can be illustrated by a report sent in 1683 to the viceroy by the chief executive of New Mexico. Governor Jironza wrote from Paso del Norte, now Ciudad Juárez, that a Jumano Indian, who became known as Don Juan Sabeata, had just come and told him of many tribes to the eastward who had sent to ask for missionaries. Among the thirty-three groups that he named was the "gran Reyno de los Texas," some fifteen or twenty days eastward from the mouth of the Conchos River, Sabeata's home. This populous country was ruled by a powerful "king." It lay beyond the Aijados[3] and was next-door neighbor to

[2] According to Fray Alonso de Paredes, "Ynforme hecho a su Magd., c. 1686," AGN, Historia, vol. 3, fols. 1–18, Juan de Oñate set out from Santa Fe in 1606 with 800 men and went eastward 300 leagues to the Aijados, who had for neighbors on the north the "nación Quivera" and on the east the "Tejas"; ibid., fol. 9. The same authority tells us that in 1606 Captain Diego del Castillo went with 8 soldiers from Santa Fe 200 leagues southeastward to the river called the Nueces, apparently the upper of the middle Colorado, and remained six months with the Jumanos, who lived there. Going down the Nueces to the southeast, they reached the Escanjaques and Aijados, and 50 leagues farther on they came to the edge of the "nación que llaman Tejas." A tradition later grew up in New Mexico that Castillo had been king of the Texas. See Governor Domingo Jironza Pétriz de Cruzate to Viceroy Marqués de la Laguna, Santa Fe, October 30, 1683, AGN, Provincias Internas, vol. 35, fols. 72–74. Again, on the authority of Paredes we learn that in 1654 Diego de Guadalaxara went with 30 soldiers and some 250 Christian Indians, from Santa Fe to the Jumana, on the same "Río de las Noeses." Some of his party, under Andrés López, went 30 leagues farther east, where they had a battle with the Cuitaos, Escankaquez, and Aijados, in the country of the first-named tribe. Juan Domingo de Mendoza, who led the expedition of 1683–84, was with Guadalaxara's party. Paredes, "Ynforme . . ."

[3] The Aijados seen by Oñate, Castillo, and Guadalaxara have been identified with the Ais, or Eyeish, but with little ground, it would seem. According to the accounts of all of these expeditions they lived west of the Texas, and according to those of the last two they seem to have lived near the

Gran Quivira, so close, indeed, that the people of the two realms visited back and forth almost daily. Jironza asked permission to embrace the enticing opportunity to send an expedition to the interior and with a touch of flattery added that he would be highly gratified if through him and in the present viceroy's day "another New World" might be discovered and "two realms with two more crowns" be added to the Lord's dominions.[4]

The desired expedition was sent out in 1683–84 under Juan Domingo de Mendoza, but, although it penetrated far into the interior, reaching the upper Colorado River, it seems that it failed to reach the great kingdom of the Texas.[5] As used by Juan Sabeata and as understood by Mendoza, judging from the contents of his affidavits and his diary, the "gran Reyno de los Texas" was localized at some place eastward of the point reached by the expedition and the term applied to settled Indians who extensively practiced agriculture.

Massanet, father of the Texas missions, tells us that it was the stories of Gran Quivira and of "the kingdoms of Ticlas, Theas, and Caburcol," handed down from the mouth of the Venerable María Jesús de Ágreda that attracted him from

---

middle Colorado or Brazos. Father Nícolas López, who was with the Mendoza expedition in 1683–84, says that he entered the "lands of the tribe that they call Aijados, next to the great kingdom of Quivira" but that he did not reach the "Kingdom of the Texas"; Domingo de Mendoza, Representación, March 26, 1686, AGN, Historia, vol. 298, fol. 74. Since it is evident that López did not reach the Brazos and that at this time the Ais were living east of the Texas, beyond the Angelia River, we must conclude that the Indians that López called the Aijados, whoever they were, were not the Ais. See Frederick Webb Hodge, ed. *Handbook of the American Indian North of Mexico*, Bureau of American Ethnology Bulletin no. 30 (1907), 1: 448–49.

[4]Cruzate to Laguna, fols. 72–74.

[5]Unprinted map made by Father Pichardo on the basis of an extended study of the original sources shows Mendoza's route as running down the Rio Grande about halfway from El Paso to Eagle, then eastward, passing north of San Saba, across the little Brazos. My opinion is that the place reached was probably on the upper Colorado, far west of the point marked by Pichardo.

Spain to the western wilds;[6] and when in 1689 he went with Alonso de León to find La Salle's establishment, he was preoccupied with this notion. On the way they were greeted by Indians with what Massanet understood to be the words "techas! techas!"[7] Near the Colorado River they were met by the chief of the Nabedache, the westernmost tribe of the Hasinai group, and in the next year they established a mission at this chief's village, west of the Neches River.[8] They must have heard while there that the local group name Hasinai, or Asinai, for this designation, rendered Cenis, is the only name given to this village by La Salle's party, who had been there only a few months before, and was later reported as the true name by one of Massanet's companions. Yet both Massanet and De León, prepossessed it would seem, with the notion of a great kingdom of the Texas, and thinking or wishing it understood that they had found it, wrote of this chief as the "governor" and of his people as the Texas.[9]

From the standpoint of the Indians whom Massanet and De León called Texas, both of these designations were misleading, as was soon shown by Fray Francisco Casañas, who was left by Massanet with the Nabedaches. After more than a year's residence among them Casañas wrote at his mission his precious Relación of August 15, 1691. In it he emphatically asserted that, contrary to the prevailing notion, the Indian

[6] Damián Massanet, "Carta de Don Damian Mazanet a Don Carlos de Siguenza y Góngora sobre el Descubrimiento de la Bahia de Espiritu Santo," trans. Lilia M. Casis, Quarterly of the Texas State Historical Association 2 (April, 1899): 282. For the legends concerning this woman see Edmond J. P. Schmidt, 'Ven. María Jesús de Agreda: A Correction," Quarterly of the Texas State Historical Association 1 (October, 1897): 121–24. See also Massanet, "Carta," pp. 255, 280, 282, 312.

[7] Ibid., p. 286. It is to be noted that this welcome was received far west of the Hasinai country, apparently extended by non-Caddoan Indians.

[8] For data on this location see below.

[9] Massanet, "Carta," p. 286. For Massanet's argument intended to prove that these Indians had been visited by the Venerable María Jesús de Agreda, see ibid., p. 312. This belief was made light of by a witness at least as trustworthy, one of Massanet's companions.

tribes about him did not constitute a kingdom; that the chief called "governor" by Massanet and De León was not head chief, and that the name of the immediate group of nine tribes was not Texas, but Aseney. "Texias," he explained, agreeing with Massanet, meant "friends" and was a general name applying to a large group of tribes, some fifty or more in number, who were customarily allied. They included tribes speaking several entirely different languages and living as far apart as the Rio Grande and the Red River.

To give his own words, Casañas says:

Let me note that this name of Texias applies to all the friendly tribes, although their languages may be different. And the reason why this name is common is no other than that of their long-standing friendship. Hence among all these tribes Texias means "friends." These friends do not all have one man, as a kingdom usually has, who governs them and whom we call king. They have only a Chenesi, who is usually a person who embraces in his government four or five tribes, which, taken together, would form a province. Kingdom this might be called, and a very large one, if these friendly tribes had a head who governs them all. But this they have not, and thus I conclude that this province, which in New Spain they call Texias, cannot be called a kingdom. They say very appropriately that they were Texias, because they are friends of all the rest. The proper name of this province is Aseney. It is composed of the nine tribes already enumerated.

They were the Nabadachos, Nechas, Nechauis, Nacachaus, Nazadachotzis, Cachaes, Nabitis, and the Nasayayas. "Only one of these nine tribes is not Aseney," he adds, "but is united with the other eight. The friendly tribes, who for another name are called Texias, are the following." Hereupon he gives a list, faulty, perhaps, of some forty-eight tribes, exclusive of some of the Hasinais. Twenty-one of them are north and east of the mission at the Neches where he is writing. Five of these twenty-one compose the "very large province" of "los Cadodachos," on the Red River. Eighteen are to the southwest and nine to the northeast. One tribe, the Chumans, of the Rio Grande and Upper Colorado country, we recognize as the

Jumanos, and from other sources we know that Casañas is correct in calling them friends of the Hasinais.[10] Continuing, our author tells us that the "province of Aseney," in whose midst the missions are located and "which in New Spain they call Texias," begins about twelve leagues east of the Trinity River and lies in the valleys of the rivers Archangel San Miguel (Neches)[11] and the Pasqua de Espíritu Santo (Angelina), extending over a territory some thirty-five leagues in length.[12]

From the standpoint of the Indians among whom he was writing, this statement by Casañas seems to be essentially correct. It is the most authoritative single account that has come to light, and it is supported by much of the related evidence. On the first point, that the native name of the local group was Hasinai (Aseney, Asinay), and that Texas was but a secondary and descriptive designation attached to them from the outside, there seems little room for doubt. The geographical extent of the application of the name Hasinai is not so clear.

Some of the data supporting the testimony of Casañas must

[10] Fray Francisco de Jesús María Casañas, Relación, August 15, 1691, AGN, Historia, vol. 394, fols. 3, 12. The following is the list. In one or two cases it is doubtful whether a given word is a compound tribal name or stands for two distinct tribes. Consequently it is impossible to say exactly how many tribes he names. The friendly tribes: Nazonis, Nacaus, Nadaydachos, Neitas, Guascos, Catayes, Neticatzis, Nasayayas, Nauitis, Caxo Dostones, Nadous, Tadiuas, Nabeyxas, Nacoz, Cayniguas, Cadaudachos, Quizis, Natzoos, Nasitoxes, Bideys, Guazas and Aduzas, Batas, Cojos, Datanas, Chumans, Cagayas, Asseneys (distinct from the Aseneys, he says), Caquizas, Quiutcanuahas, Caais, Tinibas, Vidixes, Sicos, Toahas, Cantouhaonas, Mepayayas, Canonidibas, Casibas, Dicos, Xannas, Vintas, Tobos, Caquixas, Daquixes, Canonizos, Chitouis, Zonomis. The enemies of the Hasinais: Anaos, Tanicos, Quibagas, Canzas, Ayxes, Nauydixes, Nabitis, Nondacaus, Quitxixes, Zauanitos, Tanqua ays, Cana ba tinu quiguayas, Diu Juans, Sadammos (Apaches) Caau cozis, Manis. See ibid., fol. 109. It seems quite certain that in some cases he gave wrong locations and that he placed some of the tribes in the wrong class.

[11] This stream was given the name Archangel San Miguel by Alonso De León in 1690.

[12] It may be noted that the ordinary Spanish league was about two miles.

be included even in a summary sketch. To begin with negative evidence, it is significant that the several chroniclers of the La Salle expedition to the tribes in question did not once, to my knowledge, use the name Texas in their voluminous reports, but designated the two main Caddoan groups they encountered as the Cenis (Hasinais) and Kadohadachos (Cadodaquious). I attribute this divergence from the reports of Massanet and de Leon to the fact that the La Salle party were ignorant of the Mexican rumors of the "Gran Reyno de los Texas." Of the well-known French explorers who reported upon the Indians of northeast Texas after La Salle's expedition and before St. Denis went to Mexico (1714), none, I believe, used the name Texas. The list includes Tonty, Iberville, Bienville, and the Talons, who were left by Joutel and who lived some time among the Hasinais.[13]

Returning now to positive evidence, we find much that supports Casañas's statements. Terán led the first important Spanish expedition after the founding of the missions. He set out, as he wrote, to explore the "kingdom of the Texas," but before he returned to Mexico he abandoned the name Texas, except as an alternative or an official designation, while in his report he gave us new light on the usage of the word. It is interesting to follow the unfolding of his ideas. In the first entry in his diary, following the terminology of his instructions, which had not used the term "Hasinai," Terán declares his intention to find "the kingdom of the Tejas and other provinces."[14] On the way northeast he once more refers to this kingdom of the Texas.[15] But as soon as he crosses the Trinity into the Hasinai country, he learns their distinctive name and drops the other. As he approaches the Nabedache village, when speaking of

[13] Benjamin F. French, ed., *Historical Collections of Louisiana*, 1: 74; for the Talons see Pierre Margry, ed. and trans., *Découvertes et éstablissements des français dans l'ouest et dans le sud de l'Amérique Septentrionale, 1614–1754*, 3: 610–21; for Iberville and Bienville see ibid., 4: 331, 336, 401, 432, 434.

[14] Terán, "Derrotero," fol. 23.

[15] Ibid., fol. 27.

the kingdom of the Texas, or the Teija,[16] he considers it necessary to explain that "this tribe is called by the natives Asinay, or Teija, which in their language means 'friend'." The country of the Hasinai he pompously calls "El Nuevo Reyno de la Nueva Montaña de Santander y Santillana" or "Montaña de Santander y Santillana, Provincia de la Nación Asinay." After reaching the Nabedache, he at least eight times calls the immediate group of tribes the Asinay, but apparently never once the Texas.[17]

This alone is enough to show that Terán's conversion from Texas to Asinay was complete, but there is still stronger evidence. All through the scores of folios of the *autos* written during this expedition, Asinay was used to the exclusion of Texas as a tribal name. In these documents several witnesses subscribe, under oath, to the statement that "the Asinay tribe" cannot be the kingdom of the Texas described by the Venerable María Jesús de Ágreda. That kingdom, they say, must be farther north—*mas allá*. As for the name Texas they declare that "the said Asinay tribe, in their own language, call one another and even us, when talking to us, Texas, which means 'friends'; that the tribe is Asinay; that all this is so well understood through having seen it and experienced it whenever on talking to them the Indians wished to salute them."[18]

In the next period of Spanish occupation, the early eighteenth century, the testimony is similar. St. Denis's Declaración given in Mexico in 1715 shows his preference for Asinay over Texas by his using ordinarily the former alone or the designation "Asinay alias Texas." When the form "Texas" is first introduced by him, it is explained. Since the French writers had not hitherto used the name "Texas"; since Penicaut in his account of this expedition does not use the name "Texas"

[16] The Historia copy of Terán gives "Teysa," ibid., fol. 33.
[17] Ibid., fols. 33, 45, 46, 48, 55, 57, 60, 61, 71.
[18] Terán, "Autos of the Terán expedition" (August 22, 1691—March 21, 1692), AGN, Provincias Internas, vol. 182, fol. 56.

once, but frequently calls the Indians in question Assinais;[19] and particularly since our primary version of the Declaración is a Spanish translation made in Mexico, one wonders if the "alias Texas" is not a Spanish interpolation.

The missionary fathers who accompanied St. Denis and Ramón to establish the missions in 1716, in their joint Certificación refer to their foundations as "these missions of the province of N. P. San Francisco de los Asinay (*vulgo* Texas)," while in their Representación they report having arrived at this "desired province of Asinay, or Texas."[20] Father Espinosa, who signed both of the documents last cited, in his diary of the same expedition seems to use Asinay and Texas as synonymous.[21] But in his *Chrónica Apostólica*, written after several years' residence among them, he designates them as "Assinais, called Texas," or known as Texas; explains, like Casañas and Terán before him, and like Solís, [Governor Jacinto] Barrios [Jáuregui] and numerous others after him, that "Texia . . . in the Assinais language means friends;" and implies that this fact accounts for their being accidentally called Texas.[22] Nothing could be more conclusive.

One other explanation of the word Texas deserves especially to be noted, because it makes clearer its more technical usage in the sense of allies and also reveals the persistence of its employment in this sense by the natives during a century of contact with the French and the Spaniards. Athanase de Mézières, in his day and [jurisdiction] the dean of Indian

[19] St. Denis, "Declaration by Saint Denis made in Mexico (1715)," AGN, Historia, vol. 27, fols. 121–26; Margry, ed. and trans., *Découvertes* 4: 214–21. The latter version of the "Declaration" is evidently a retranslation into French. Penicaut, "Relation," in ibid., 5: 499–502.

[20] "Certificación by the missionaries in Texas," July 22, 1716, AGN, Historia, vol. 27, fol. 162.

[21] Isidro Felix de Espinosa, Diario, 1716, AGN, Historia, vol. 394, fol. 134.

[22] Isidro Felix de Espinosa, *Chrónica apostólica, y seráphica de todos los colegios de propaganda fide de esta Nueva-España*, p. 408.

agents, wrote in 1778 that the best way to bring the Comanches to Spanish allegiance would be to attach them, in the honorable position of allies, to a campaign he was proposing to make against the Apaches, in company with the principal tribes of northeastern Texas, "because," he explained, "from such a custom comes the name of Techán among[23] the natives, which is similar to [alude á] that of commilito, with which the Romans flattered themselves, and results in a close tie of friendship among those who call themselves by this name and in the popular opinion that no one may break it without fearing and incurring the penalty merited by perjurers."[24] There can be little doubt that the word rendered Techán by Mézières was the same as the forms Texias, Texas, Techas, Teyas, etc., which much earlier was explained as meaning "allies".

From all this and much more evidence of a like nature which might be adduced, it is plain that Hasinai was the native name for these tribes of the Neches and Angelina valleys among whom the Spaniards founded their establishments. It need only be added that Hasinai is the group name by which their descendants still call themselves today.

Nevertheless, through an erroneous preconception, strengthened by the first reports of Massanet and De León, Texas became the official designation of the province, and this latter fact primarily caused the same name instead of the more correct one to be fastened upon the Neches-Angelina people. Eye-witnesses continued to write that Hasinai was the correct general name of the Indians about the east Texas missions, but the officials in Mexico persisted in designating them as the Texas and narrowed this broad term to include only a few tribes. Velasco, the royal fiscal, for example, in his Resumen Arreglado, written November 30, 1716, summarizing and

[23] It is to be noted that the accents used by Mézières in this and accompanying letters are French accents, indicating quantity, not stress.

[24] Athanasio de Mézières to Teodoro de Croix, February 20, 1779, AGN, Historia, vol. 28, fol. 235.

paraphrasing many of the earlier reports, palpably ignores the name Hasinai and, whenever he finds it, substitutes Texas, except in one instance where the Hasinais are erroneously given as a subtribe of the Texas.[25]

In this way, through the weight of official authority, Texas came to be employed during most of the eighteenth century as the more usual name for the Hasinai group, and from the Spaniards the name was borrowed by French and English. As a tribal name it was sometimes still further narrowed to designate the head tribe of the Hasinai confederacy, whose correct name was well known to be Hainai. Still later it was sometimes applied exclusively to the Nabedache tribe, the westernmost of the confederacy. On the other hand, when missionary and political activity extended westward to the San Antonio and La Vaca regions, Texas, as a geographical term, was extended, more in harmony with its use by the natives, to all of the country between the Medina and the Sabine rivers. Later days witnessed a still wider application, until the imperial realm of Texas embraces all the country from Texarkana to El Paso.

Recapitulating, the testimony of the sources warrants the conclusion that the word Texas, variously employed by early writers, had wide currency among the tribes of eastern Texas before the coming of the Europeans; and its most usual meaning there was "friends," or, more technically, "allies;" and that it was used, by the Hasinais at least (to whom it later became attached as a group name), to designate a large number of tribes, both Caddoans and non-Caddoans, who were customarily allied against the Apaches. In this latter sense Texas would mean little more than the group of common enemies of the Apaches. Evidently the Hasinais did not apply the term restrictively to themselves as a group name, but, on the other

[25] Velasco, "Resumen arreglado à lo que constra de los autos que se han formado en este Supr Govno de las noticias que desde el ano de 1688 asta el presents mes, y ano, se han tenido de la nacion Asinay o Texas, sus propriedades, y costumbres, . . ." AGN, Historia, vol. 27, fol. 190.

hand, they did use it in a less technical way as an everyday form of greeting, such as "Hello, friend." The Spanish narrowing of the term Texas as a group name to the tribes of the Neches and Angelina valleys is probably due to the historical circumstance that this was the first great group of allies, or "Texas," in that region, whom they came to know intimately. They were influenced, however, by an apparent but unexplained partial narrowing of the term by the Indians of western Texas from whom they first heard it.

In this connection I ought to say that the meanings "land of flowers," "tiled roofs," "paradise," etc., sometimes given for the name "Texas," I have never seen even suggested by firsthand observers. They seem to be baseless fictions of recent date.[26]

Evidence regarding the usage and meaning of the name Hasinai is equally explicit. While Texas, or Texias, as used by the Indians of eastern Texas, was thus apparently a broad and indefinite term applied to many and unrelated tribes occupying a very large area, Hasinai, on the other hand, was ordinarily used by the early writers to apply to only a portion of the Caddoan Indians of eastern Texas, the southern portion, or those living mainly in the upper Neches and Angelina valleys.

The fact that the survivors of most of the former Caddoan tribes of eastern Texas, northern and southern alike, now living together on the reservations, apply the name Hasinai collectively to their group, has led to the supposition that at the opening of the historical period it applied similarly to all

---

[26] It happens that Casañas makes a statement that conclusively proves that the name could have no connection with tiled roots or tiling. In describing the country of the Hasinais he says "There are many clay beds from which the Indians make pretty pots, and I think that, since they make pots, they might also make roof tiles (*tejas*) and brick." Casañas, Relación, fol. 3. This shows that he had never seen any roof tiles of their make. It may be added that none of the eyewitnesses whose writings I have seen ever mentioned tiled roofs among the Hasinais, but the grass-covered lodges are frequently noted.

of the tribes, northern as well as southern, now represented by these fragments in Oklahoma. Thus [James] Mooney included in the Caddo Confederacy, with the generic name Hasinai, the Caddos proper (Kadohadachos), Anadarkos (Nadakos), Ionis (Hainais), Nabedachos, Nacogdoches, Adais (Adaes), Eyeish (Ais), and Yatasses.[27] A study of contemporary evidence, however, shows that at the first coming of the Europeans, and for a long time thereafter, writers quite generally made a distinction between the northern and the southern Caddos and that only a part of the tribes just enumerated were ordinarily classed as Hasinais. These two groups were separated by a wide stretch of uninhabited territory extending between the upper Angelina and the Red River near Texarkana and were clearly distinguished by numerous French and Spanish writers. Their separateness of organization was positively affirmed, the details of the inner organization of both groups were more or less fully described, and in their relations with the Spaniards and the French they were dealt with for a century or more as separate units.

Some of the evidence on these points may be noted here. As to the first, it is noticeable that between the Nasonis, on the upper Angelina, and the Kadohadachos, chief tribe of the Red River Caddo group, a stretch of a hundred miles or more, the early diaries do not note a single village. Joutel's narrative for this part of the journey of the La Salle party is lacking, but neither [Anastase] Douay, [Claude] Delisle, nor [M. de] Michel mentions any settlements on this route. Delisle merely states that just before reaching the Red River the Nasoni guide named several tribes to the right and left, but the only names recorded are those of tribes far out of the path.[28] Douay says that Joutel's party passed the Haquis, Nabiris, and Naansis, all numerous tribes at war with the Cenis. Evidently these were passed at some distance, for, if they were enemies, they could hardly have been near the customary trial between the friendly

[27] Mooney, *The Ghost-Dance Religion*, p. 1092.
[28] Margry, ed. and trans., *Découvertes*, 3: 414.

Kadohadachos and Hasinais.[29] Terán, the Spaniard, whose diary is detailed, mentions no Indians on his way to the Kadohadachos. On the way back he once mentions meeting a few Indians, but nowhere does he mention villages or tribes between the Nasonis and the Kadohadachos. All of these writers speak of these two tribes as adjacent stations on the way, and the impression gained from these early sources is not modified by later ones, such as La Harpe's *Journal*. From this it would appear that whatever general organization the Neches-Angelina tribes and the Red River tribes may have belonged to in common, they were at least physically quite distinct and separated by a long stretch of uninhabited country.

These chroniclers of the La Salle expedition, who give us our first intimate knowledge of the Indians of northeastern Texas, all treat as distinct groups the tribes of the Neches-Angelina country and those they visited on the Red River. They restrict to the former group the name Hasinai, written by them Coenis and Cenis, while they call the Red River tribes collectively Caddaquis, or Cadodaquious. They even distinguish a third group, the Assonis (Nasonis) on the upper Angelina, but it seems from later sources that these already belonged to or soon after joined the southern confederacy.[30] Spanish testimony is similar. De León reported two groups, a northern and a southern, and called them Texas and Cadodachos. The general impression gained by these earliest writers was confirmed by a better informed witness, Casañas, who, in terms distinguishes between the "province of Aseney" and the "province of the Cadodachos." Moreover, he enumerates the individual tribes of each of these two provinces and describes in some detail the inner organization of the southern group.[31]

In 1691–92 Terán led an expedition to the Red River to verify rumors of Frenchmen in that vicinity and to become

[29] French, ed. *Historical Collections*, 4: 217.
[30] Ibid., pp. 204, 221; Margry, ed. and trans., *Découvertes*, 3: 340, 344, 408; 4: 316.
[31] Casañas, Relación, fol. 2.

acquainted with the natives and the country. The reports of this journey make the same distinction between the Kadohadachos and the Hasinais and contain evidence that the two groups had parallel inner organization.[32] Terán explicitly states, on the word of his Indian guide, that the Hasinai settlement extended only to the Nasonis, on the upper Angelina.[33] That he did not regard the Kadohadachos as Hasinais is clear from numerous other statements. For example, on December 5, 1691, he determined to leave the "Nación Cadodachos" and to return to the "Nación Asinay."[34] This discrimination of names is all the more convincing when we know that Terán remarked upon the close interrelations of the groups. Moreover, the *autos* of the Terán expedition frequently draw contrasts between the "Nación Cadodachos" and the "Nación Asinay." Finally, as for Terán and his party, they several times note for Cadodachos a Chenesi, or Teneci, parallel with that functioning at the head of the "province of the Asinays."[35] With regard to the application of the word "Asinai," Espinosa is self-contradictory and inconclusive, but in describing the tribes on the Neches and Angelina he treats the Kadohadachos under foreign relations, in the same category as the tribes of the Gulf of Mexico.[36] St. Denis and Father [Francisco] Hidalgo quite emphatically include the Kadohadachos under the Hasinais,[37] but apart from these instances the early custom is generally to the contrary.

[32] Terán, Descripción, fol. 47; Alonso de Rivera, Declaración, Real de Santa María, March 18, 1692, AGN, Historia, vol. 27, fol. 83; Terán, "Autos," fols. 66, 76, 86, 90.

[33] At a distance of seven leagues northeast of the place where he crossed the Neches he wrote that the rancherías were "las últimas de esta nación Asinay, segun noticia del Yndio originario de esta Nueva Montana." See Terán, "Descripción," fol. 49. After going five leagues farther and passing some rancherias, which, he said, were just like those of the Asinays, he apparently entered the main village of the Nasonis.

[34] Ibid., fols. 56–57.

[35] Rivera, *Declaración*, fol. 83; Terán, "Autos," fols. 60, 66, 76, 86, 96.

[36] Espinosa, *Chrónica*, p. 437.

[37] St. Denis, "Declaration," fols. 212–16.

In conclusion, while it may be impossible to determine the exact native usage of the word "Hasinai" in the seventeenth century, and while its usage by early writers was not consistent, some things are clear: (1) regardless of names, there was a very general recognition of separate organizations for the Kadohadacho group of Caddos and that in the Neches-Angelina valleys, corresponding with their geographical separation, (2) the name "Hasinai," when used by the early Spanish and French writers was most commonly employed to indicate the southern group, (3) this usage of the name was nearly or quite identical with the more ordinary Spanish usage of the word "Texas," and (4) while, for reasons explained above, Texas was the term more frequently employed to designate the group, there is a clear recognition of the fact that Hasinai is preferable from the native point of view.

The present common use of the name Hasinai by the survivors of both these groups may be explained by nineteenth-century conditions. Then the group organizations, always subject to frequent changes, apparently broke down, the tribes reorganizing in a loose way as a single group. Then it was, perhaps, that the common name Hasinai was adopted by the remains of all the tribes.

The name Hasinai, like Texas, was sometimes narrowed in its application to one tribe. Usually when this occurred the Hainai, or head tribe of the Hasinais, was designated. But sometimes the notion appears that there was a Hasinai tribe distinct from the Hainais. This, however, does not seem to have been the case. Illustrations of both these points will appear further on.

Among the surviving Texas Caddoans the word Hasinai now means "Our Own Folk!" The forms the name Hasinai has been given are interesting.[38] The earliest French writers, the chroniclers of the La Salle expedition, who visited these Indians in 1686–87, called them Coenis and Cenis. The first

[38] Mooney, *The Ghost-Dance Religion*, p. 1092. This authority says that it is also used by them to signify "Indians."

68

Spanish use of the word that I find is in the Relación of Casañas.[39] He writes the name Acenay, Asenay, Assenay, Aseney,
Asseney, and perhaps other ways. He sometimes accents and
even separates the initial syllable, which Joutel and Douay
omit entirely. Terán commonly used the form Asinay. This
form and Assinay became the most common Spanish spellings
of the word and were approximated later by French writers,[40]
whereas the earlier ones had left off the first syllable. Mooney,
who knew intimately the survivors of these people, and whose
opinion with respect to the native pronunciation may be
taken as authoritative, wrote the name by which they now
call themselves—Hasinais or Hasinis, preferably the former.
This goes to show that the Spanish writers in both the first
and the last syllable represented the native name more accu-
rately than the French.

[39] Casañas, Relación, fols. 1, 11 (Asenay).
[40] Penicaut gives the term "Assinais" in Margry, ed. and trans., Découvertes, 4: 409; La Harpe likewise gives this form in ibid., 3: 461. A
French "Memoire of 1690" gives "Senys" in ibid., 4: 319.

3

Social and Political Organization

Our fullest information concerning the social and political institutions of the Caddoan tribes relates to the Hasinais, and we may describe their local arrangements as typical of the whole Caddoan group, for all evidence available points to great similarity between the two divisions.

The Household

The visible unit of the Hasinai villages was the household group. The houses were built for communal living, each being occupied by several families. Joutel tells us in one place that there were "ordinarily eight or ten families in these cabins [cabanas]," in another, that in some of them there were "fifteen or twenty" families; and again, referring specifically to the Nasonis, that there were in each lodge "several families." To accommodate so many persons, lodges were sometimes sixty feet in diameter.[1] Massanet reported ten beds in the house of his host, a chief of the Nabedache tribe and said that the domestic work was performed by ten women each week.[2]

[1] Pierre Margry, *Découvertes et éstablissements des français dans l'ouest et dans le sud de l'Amérique Septentrionale, 1614–1754*, 3: 345, 393.

[2] Fray Damián Massanet, "Carta de Don Damian Mazanet a Don Carlos de Siguenza y Góngora Sobre el Descubrimiento de la Bahia de Espiritu Santo," trans. Lilia M. Casis, *Quarterly* of the Texas State Historical Association 2 (April, 1899): 304.

Father Douay agrees with Joutel on the size of some of the houses but says that each held two families.[3] The truth probably lies somewhere between these estimates.[4] It is thus evident that among the Hasinai communal dwellings were the rule, as was the case among most of the Indians of the continent.[5]

Communal Life

Unfortunately our authorities, not appreciating the fundamental differences between civilized and primitive communities, left little direct record of the underlying relations of the families comprised within these household groups, or of the household to the larger units of the social organization. However some of these relations appear from incidental information even though not so clearly as we might wish.

If Joutel understood what he saw, there was evidently within these lodges a well-marked balance between communal and family life. He tells us that inside the lodges were arranged to accommodate separate families, each of which had its private nook or corner, beds, and utensils. According to him the family compartments were not partitioned off, but Father Massanet (1690) tells us that in the house of his host the beds were separated by mats.[6] Joutel writes that, besides its private nook and utensils, each family of the household had its separate casks of corn or other food supply, but that one woman had charge of the food and distributed it to the rest.[7] The person whom he called *"la maîtresse des femmes"* at the house of the Nasoni chief where he stayed several days was an old woman, and was, he thought, the mother of the host.[8]

[3] Benjamin F. French, ed., *Historical Collections of Louisiana,* 4: 204.

[4] James Mooney to Bolton, April 23, 1908, Bolton Correspondence, "In."

[5] See Lewis H. Morgan, "House and House-Life of the American Aborigines," *Contributions to North American Ethnology* 4 (1881).

[6] French, ed., *Historical Collection,* p. 148; Massanet, "Carta," p. 303.

[7] Margry, ed. and trans., *Découvertes,* 3: 393. From the language used by Joutel, one could not say whether "each" (*chacun*) modifies "family" or "person."

[8] Ibid.

On the other hand, the fire was used by the whole household, and even though there were individual utensils, some at least of the cooking was done in common. We are told, for instance, that in making their sagamite, or porridge, one of their principal dishes, each family [9] furnished from its private stock its quota of corn or flour, but that all was put together and cooked by one person and when ready was distributed by the head woman. [10] One witness went so far as to say in one place that it seemed that they had no private property; but in another he contradicts himself by stating that they had personal possessions, such as clothing, etc. [11] Thus within these communal dwellings community life was balanced by individual and family activity. It will be seen further on, when we come to discuss economic life, that in the more difficult tasks community labor extended to the whole village group, or even to several villages. This was true of preparing the ground for the seed, of house building, and of going on the long and dangerous buffalo and bear hunts. It goes without saying that religious and social activities were mainly communal.

Clans

A clan organization, it is clear, existed among the Hasinais, but of the details of the grouping we know very little. The clans were evidently exogamous, for [Fray Juan Agustín] Morfí writes, "Affinity is not an impediment to marriage, but consanguinity is a very great one and [marriage within it] is scrupulously avoided." [12] Such direct evidence as there is all points

[9] Here again the substantive to which *chacun* refers is indefinite but is apparently *famille*.

[10] Margry, ed. and trans., *Découvertes*, 3: 303. Compare this arrangement with Lucien Carr, "On the Social and Political Position of Women among the Huron-Iroquois Tribes," *Reports of the Peabody Museum* 3 (1880–86): 215.

[11] Fray Francisco de Jesús María Casañas, Relación, August 15, 1691, AGN, Historia, vol. 394, fol. 8.

[12] Fray Juan Agustín Morfí, "Historia de Texas," trans. F. F. Hilder, MS 1750, National Anthropological Archives, Smithsonian Institution, bk. 3, p. 103.

to the paternal rather than to the maternal basis of the clans. Thus, though we are not clearly informed whether a man married into the family of his wife or took his wife home with him, the inference from what Casañas tells us (1691) is that the latter was the case.[13] Espinosa and Casañas both inform us, too, that consent to marry a maiden but not a widow was obtained by the man from the girl's father or brother, rather than from a female head of the family.[14] The little light we get on inheritance indicates that it was in the male line. This was true of tribal chieftainship, for example, but Morfí tells us also that a man inherited his deceased brother's wife, whether she had children or not.[15] These facts all seem to indicate father-right instead of mother-right in the family organization.

Mooney tells us, on the basis of a study of the survivors on their reservation in western Oklahoma, that the Caddos now have ten *gentes:* Bear (*Nawotsi*), Wolf (*Tasha*), Buffalo (*Tánaha*), Beaver (*Táo*), Eagle (*Iwi*), Raccoon (*O-at*), Crow (*Ká g'aih*), Thunder (*Ká-ga hanin*), Panther (*Kcshi*), Sun (*Sûko*). It is true that the survivors represent mainly the Kadohadacho and Nadako dialects, but it may also be true that the *gentes* named were common to the other tribes.[16] Some of them evidently were. In 1763 Barthélemy de Macarty, commandant at Natchitoches, wrote as a proof of the common descent of the Caddo tribes,—enumerating the Caodachos, Nazones, Nacogdoches, Acinays (Hainais), Yatassez, and Natchitoches— that they all spoke the same idiom and were divided into four families, namely the Beaver, the Otter, the Wolf, and the Lion.[17] To make these names correspond with Mooney's list

[13] Casañas, Relación, fol. 8.

[14] Isidro Felix de Espinosa, *Chrónica apostólica, y seráphica de todos los colegios de propaganda fide de esta Nueva-España,* p. 427.

[15] Morfí, "Historia," p. 103.

[16] James Mooney, "The Caddo and Associate Tribes," in *The Ghost-Dance Religion,* Fourteenth Annual Report of the Bureau of American Ethnology (1896), 2: 1093.

[17] Chevalier Barthélemy de Macarty to Governor Ángel de Martos de Navarrete, November 17, 1763, Nacogdoches Archives, State Library, Austin, Texas.

we would have to change Macarty's Otter to Raccoon and his Lion to Panther. Whether Macarty's list of only four groups is an evidence of his ignorance as to the number of clans or is an indication of a larger grouping of clans into phratries I cannot say. His classification may have corresponded to the grouping for religious and ceremonial purposes that is indicated below. On the relation of the clan to the grouping of the households into villages, or on the other hand, of the clan to the tribal organization, I have no light other than that shed by analogy, upon which I shall base no conjecture.

Tribal Government of the Caddis

When we come to tribal organization, we are on surer ground. Each of the tribes belonging to the confederacy had regularly a separate government, at the head of which was a civil chief called *caddi*.[18] The Kadohadacho tribes called their chiefs by the same name. According to Joutel this word was pro-nounced *cä-ä-di*, but in Espinosa's *Chrónica* we find it ac-cented on the last syllable, thus, *caddí*.[19]

In the civil and religious affairs of the tribe these chiefs seem to have been more than ordinarily powerful. This would be indicated indeed, by the fact that the office of caddi was held for life and was hereditary,[20] which was by no means the universal rule among the Texas tribes.[21] The succession might

[18] We learn, as an instance of the union of different tribes under one chief, that in 1752–53 the same person was chief of the Nasonis and the Nadotes (Nadocos?). See Manuel Antonio de Soto Bermudez, Investiga-ción, November 12, 1752, AGN, Provincias Internas, vol. 181, fol. 134.

[19] Margry, ed. and trans., *Découvertes*, 3: 363; Espinosa, *Chrónica*, p. 420.

[20] Casañas, Relación, fol. 7; Fray Gaspár José de Solís, Diario, AGN, Historia, vol. 27, fol. 290, makes the offhand statement that all of the Texas tribes chose their bravest men as chiefs, but he had little acquaintance with Texas, and his word cannot stand against that of the Talons, Casañas, and Espinosa.

[21] In the related Taovaya or Wichita tribes the chiefs were elected, but the Pawnees, also related, had hereditary chiefs. See Athanase de Mézières to Viceroy Antonio Maria de Bucareli, July 4, 1772, AGN, Provincias Inter-

fall upon either the son or the nearest male relative.[22] An instance of succession in the collateral line appeared in the later eighteenth century when Bigotes, for many years chief of the Nabedache tribe, was succeeded by his brother Baltasar.[23] Sometimes an aged chief associated his son with him.[24]

In case a child inherited the office of caddi, one of the chief men took his place temporarily, acting as regent. Meanwhile the seat of honor in the council was reserved for the child, who attended the meetings, although during the deliberations he might be playing about or sleeping.[25] Espinosa tells us that the succession never caused any trouble, but we are not required to believe this to be universally true.[26]

The caddi combined the functions of a civil executive and a priest and might serve also as a war leader. On the one hand, Casañas says "He is like a governor who rules them."[27] He ruled through a council and was assisted by subordinate officers. He called the council and presided over it. He must also have supervised, either personally or through his subordinates, many details of life, for we learn, for example, that consent to build a house, or, in certain cases, to marry, was

---

nas, vol. 20, fol. 16, and Historia, vol. 51, fol. 17; John B. Dunbar, "The Pawnee Indians: Their History and Ethnology," *Magazine of American History* 4 (April, 1880): 261–62.

[22] Espinosa, *Chrónica*, p. 435; Massanet tells us in 1691 that the chief of the Kadohadachos was a boy some twelve years old, whose father had recently died. The implication clearly is that here as well as among the Hasinais the chieftainship was hereditary. Massanet Papers, AGN, Provincias Internas, vol. 182.

[23] Felipe de Neve to Domingo Cabello, Arizpe, December 26, 1783, Bexar Archives, reel 15, frames 0632–34.

[24] An instance of this is reported of the Nabedaches by the Talons; Margry, ed. and trans., *Découvertes*, 3: 617.

[25] Espinosa, *Chrónica*, p. 435. *Tonty tells us that in 1690 a woman was head of the Caddo tribe on the Red River. It may be that she was the regent mother of the boy said by Massanet to be chief in 1691.*

[26] Espinosa, *Chrónica*, p. 435.

[27] Casañas, Relación, fol. 7.

obtained from him.[28] As a priest we find him on different occasions, "blessing" food, as it were, by a peculiar religious ceremony and performing other religious rites.

In this connection, Peña (1721) records a Spanish belief in a peculiar Hasinai custom. He says that he was met at the Neches River by one hundred Macono (Nacono) Indians "and their chief, who is also head priest to their idols. He is blind, and it is presumed that after having been chief many years, his eyes were put out, as is the custom with the Indians in order to become head priest."[29] I have found no corroboration of this belief. Certain it is that some caddis performed priestly ceremonies without being blinded.

The caddi went to war, hunted, and worked in the fields like other men; yet his person had a certain sanctity about it not common to ordinary individuals, injury to his person being punished with heavier penalties than in other cases. This sanctity of person, Casañas thought, extended to his immediate family.[30]

The caddis usually had only one wife each. They were distinguished from other women by having a common name, Awuidau, while all other women had individual names.[31]

If we assume the domestic arrangements of the Nabedache tribe to have been typical, and that Massanet understood what he saw, it seems that the community was responsible for the care of the caddi's house. We are told by this witness, who was a guest of the caddi of the tribe, that "each week ten Indian women undertake the housework; each day at sunrise they come laden with firewood, sweep out the courtyard and the house, carry water from the brook, which is at some distance, and grind corn for the atole, tamales, and pinole. Each woman goes home for the night, returning to the governor's house next morning."[32]

[28] Ibid., fol. 9.
[29] Peña, Diario, fol. 36.
[30] Casañas, Relación, fols. 7–9.
[31] Ibid., fol. 7.
[32] Massanet, "Carta," p. 304.

War Chiefs

Besides these hereditary civil chief-priests there were elective war chiefs, whose authority seems to have been confined to the period of the campaign for which they were chosen. The number of war chiefs does not appear, but there are indications that each distinct portion of the tribe had one. The war chief was chosen for his valor, and he was expected, says Espinosa, not only to lead in a fight, but in case of a reverse to cover the retreat from the enemy.[33]

Espinosa makes it appear that the authority of the war chief during the campaign was absolute: "They obey him without violating his orders, in the least and even though they may have marched all day without taking food they do not even refresh the tongue on passing by a stream until the chief orders a halt."[34] There are indications, however, that this is an overstatement of the war chief's authority. Pierre Talon, who had lived several years among the Hasinais, in describing their war methods says of the chief's authority that it was "so limited that each one quits and returns to his lodge when the fancy to do so seizes him, without asking permission or consent of the commander, for they conduct war without any order or discipline."[35]

Councils

Business of importance was transacted in the councils, which were composed of the principal men. Casañas speaks of them as being made up of the elders (*los viejos*) and implies that the younger men (*mozos*) were not admitted.[36] Espinosa mentions meetings of the caddi (*capitán principal*) and the "other chiefs

[33] Espinosa, *Chrónica*, p. 435.

[34] Ibid., p. 434.

[35] Margry, ed. and trans., *Découvertes*, 3: 616. A similar lack of authority on the part of a Nassonite war chief is indicated in a passage of La Harpe's "Journal du Voyage," ibid., 4: 271.

[36] Casañas, Relación, fol. 8.

[*capitánes*] and old men."[37] The meetings were held in a council house built especially for this purpose or at the house of the caddi.[38] During the session the strictest decorum was observed, it being a breach of good manners to disturb the deliberations either from within or from without. Speech was free. Each member in turn, according to his rank, which was indicated by his seat, gave his opinion, the others meanwhile listening respectfully and giving visible signs of such attention. Casañas conveys the idea that after hearing the opinions of all, the caddi decided what was best.[39] If this be true, it indicates considerable real executive authority on the caddi's part. The evidence available does not enable us to say whether or not there were lesser councils of the clans or other divisions of the tribe.

Canahas, Chayas, and Tammas

To assist in the civil government there were administrative functionaries called *canahas* (or *cayahas*), *chayas*, and *tammas*. Casañas said that the number of the *canahas* under each caddi varied from three or four to seven or eight, depending upon the size of his district. A canaha was to the caddi both an administrative agent and a personal servant. In the former sphere he seems to have been a sort of public crier, such as [John B.] Dunbar describes among the Pawnees, who were related to the Hasinais.[40] A difference is that each Pawnee chief had one herald, while the Hasinai chiefs had several each. In the capacity of crier the canaha called the council together for business and proclaimed the will of the caddi, threatening punishment for those who might fail to obey. As a personal servant he accompanied the caddi to war or the chase, super-

[37] Espinosa, *Chrónica*, p. 436.
[38] Margry, *Découvertes*, 3: 343; Massanet, "Carta," p. 304; Casañas, Relación, fol. 7.
[39] Casañas, Relación, fols. 8, 9.
[40] Dunbar, "The Pawnee Indians," p. 262.

vised the arrangement of his lodge, and prepared his pipe and tobacco when he wished to smoke.[41]

Subject to the orders of the canahas were officers called *chayas* (singular, *chaya*). As to what they did we have no information other than the assertion that "they do whatever the cayaha [*canaha*] commands them."[42]

Of more practical importance in daily affairs were the *tammas*. These functionaries, of lower rank than the canahas, were messengers, policemen, and overseers; Espinosa calls them *procuradores* or *mandones*.[43] Casañas says "these are the ones who hasten affairs. The lazy they whip on the legs with rods or withes." They prepared materials for ceremonials, ran from hamlet to hamlet calling people together for festivals, notified them when they must help in community labor, and stood by to see that each did his own part.[44]

Punishments

To evildoers corporal punishment was freely administered according to the degree of the offense. For lesser misdemeanors delinquents were whipped by the tammas.[45] Espinosa, describing community work at housebuilding, thus spoke of minor punishments: "All this time the overseers [the tammas] with their rods of two or three flexible green branches go about hurrying the people; and the man or woman who is tardy

[41] Casañas, Relación, fol. 7.
[42] Ibid.
[43] Espinosa, *Chrónica*, p. 420.
[44] Ibid., pp. 420, 421, 431; Casañas, Relación, fol. 12. It is interesting to note that the Spanish authorities frequently mentioned *tammas* among the Arkokisa and Bidai Indians. This might indicate a similarity of language between these and the Hasinai tribes, but it probably indicates merely that the Spaniards applied a Hasinai name to a functionary among the Bidai and Arkokisa tribes similar to the *tamma*. In 1768, Solís went through the Nabedache village and in his diary mentioned there, "*tamas conas*, who are the priests and like captains among them." See Solís, Diario, fol. 281.
[45] Casañas, Relación, fol. 12.

catches it. If it is a man the overseer gives him four or five strokes with the rod across the breast; if a woman, he uncovers her shoulders and does likewise. This is done without exception as to persons; for even if it is the tamma's own wife or sister who is at fault, she gets her punishment. No one shows any sorrow over it, but instead they laugh,"[46] which of course hurts worse than the blows.

Our observers did not mention the aversion to shedding kindred blood through punishment that was frequently found among the Indian tribes.[47] We are told that a murderer of an ordinary citizen was usually beaten so hard that he did not recover; while an injury resulting in the death of a caddi or one of his family was punished with certain death. Since banishment was practiced among them, however, it is possible that the murderer was first outlawed, in order that by this fiction the shedding of kindred blood might be avoided.[48] One guilty of horse stealing might, besides being required to make reparation, be threatened with banishment, or *que se desmade*.[49] Blood vengeance was widely enforced with respect to enemies, but among themselves the Hasinais did not indulge freely in private vengeance, we are told, for they regularly took their troubles to the caddi and the council.[50]

As a commentary upon their general good government, Casañas remarked that during a fifteen months' residence among the Hasinais he had never seen disturbances any more than a stir occasioned by the punishment of some lazy or bold fellow, or by a domestic quarrel between a man and his wife. Espinosa in his writings conveys the same impression.

[46] Espinosa, *Chrónica*, p. 420.
[47] J. W. Powell, *Wyandot Government*, First Annual Report of the Bureau of American Ethnology (1881), p. 67; Livingston Farrand, *Basis of American History, 1500–1900*, p. 199.
[48] Casañas says that he never saw the death penalty invoked but that the custom was so well known that even children understood the law. Casañas, Relación, fols. 8, 9.
[49] Espinosa, *Chrónica*, p. 436.
[50] Ibid.

Confederacy Organization

Tribal bonds and tribal government were more intimate and more important than any intertribal political arrangements. Though he exaggerated, Macarty expressed a half truth when, in order to prove in a controversial letter that the Hasinais (Acinays) were not the head group of all the Caddo Indians, he said "there is no village, however weak and unhappy it may be, which is not regarded by the others as free and independent." [51] Yet, speaking relatively, the confederate relations of the tribes in the Neches-Angelina valleys were close. The basis of this grouping, however, was as much or more religious than political. For religious purposes there was first a subgrouping. Ordinarily the Neches and Hainais held their ceremonials and festivals together, while the Nacogdoches and Nazonis formed another group. [52] How the other subgroups were composed does not appear.

With the surrounding tribes the Hasinais maintained strict peace, and in case any individual violated the terms of peace agreements they sent to his tribe a messenger with the notice of the grievance. A council of chief men was called, the delinquent summoned before it, and they reprimanded him and threatened him with banishment or physical punishment, as the facts might warrant.

Many religious functions involved the whole confederacy. One tribe, the Hainai, was regarded as the head tribe, and what primarily gave it prestige was the location on its western border of the chief temple containing the sacred fire from which directly or indirectly all the households kindled their hearths and where the general religious festivals were held. [53]

[51] Chevalier Barthelemy de Macarty to Governor Ángel de Martos y Navarrete, Natchitoches, November 17, 1763, Nacogdoches Archives, Austin, Texas. A typed copy is in the Bolton Papers, Bancroft Library.

[52] Espinosa, *Chrónica*, p. 425.

[53] "La Casa del Fuego es la de los Ainais como la Parroquis o cathedral; y otro en los Naiches, y otro en los Nacodochis y Nazonis; y este fuego se llevo a aquellas Casas . . . Todas las Casas, o las de ellas, se sirven de el fuego de

The Chenesi

Presiding over this fire temple was the head priest of the confederacy, called the Chenesi. Espinosa, Casañas, and Terán agree in regarding him as the highest individual authority in the group, but they do not give the same view as to the nature of his position. Massanet, who met him at the Nabedache village, regarded him as a high priest; Espinosa considered him mainly in this light, but testified that his authority was superior to that of any chief (*capitán*); Casañas speaks of him not only as a priest but also as a "little king" and tells of his great power as a ruler.[54] Terán clearly considered him as a head chief, with direct authority over the caddis. In the diary of his expedition from the Nabedaches to the Kadohadachos he writes, just after crossing the Neches: "I may note also that from the crossing of the arroyo there is another jurisdiction with another chief [*capitán*] where he whom they call Governor has no authority [*ni bara ni mandato*] and is neither recognized nor obeyed. The chief of this division has the same authority as the other, both being equally subject to the Indian they call Cenes."[55] As for the nature of his authority over his people, Casañas remarked, "they are by nature peaceful and obedient to the orders of the Chenesi, who is a little king to them, . . . to him are subject these nine nations."[56] Again: "The respect and obedience they show the Gran Chenesi is great. They all try to be content to give him what they have and to go to hunt for things with which he may regale himself. Finally, in his government, he merely says 'I wish this or that done,' when everybody responds because of the fear of his commands." Concerning the Chenesi's superiority to the cad-

---

aquella principal Casa," Espinosa, *Chrónica*, p. 425. That the first house was on the western edge of the Hasinai territory is shown by Espinosa's statement that it was between the Hasinai and the Neches tribes. Ibid., p. 424.

[54] Casañas, Relación, fol. 10.

[55] Domingo de Terán, Diario, 1691–92, AGN, Historia, vol. 27, fol. 48.

[56] Casañas, Relación, fol. 5.

dis, Casañas is explicit. Commenting on the danger of arousing jealousies among the Indians—a mistake which De León had actually made among the Hasinais—he says:

It is desirable that he be given some presents, because he is head of all this province. He who hitherto has been given presents [the Nabedache caddi], made governor, and given the bastón is no more than a caddi, subject with the other eight of these nine tribes to the Gran Chenesi. And however much this one is regaled, it is not possible that he should cease to recognize the Chenesi as his superior. I know that it will be well to regale the Chenesi more than him. Thus all the other caddis will be very well satisfied, seeing that no one is recognized as greater than the Chenesi.[57]

Clearly Casañas regarded the Chenesi as something more than a priest. Yet, aside from these statements, the details he gives us are confined mainly to priestly functions and indicate rather a religious than a civil authority.[58] Moreover, we learn that the Hainai caddi or civil chief was regarded as the "*capitán grande,*" or head civil chief, superior to the other caddis. Thus it seems that the Chenesi was primarily a priest, but that through his personal dignity and influence he outranked all others, and that his word had great authority in civil as well as religious affairs.

The Chenesi lived, in the center of the confederacy on the edge of or within the Hainai tribe, near the Angelina River. Casañas tells us that the office of Chenesi was hereditary, and the inference from all circumstances is that it was attached to the Hainai tribe. The Chenesi's most important duty was to care for the temple near his house, where were kept the sacred flames and the *coninisi* by means of which he talked with the Great Chief above.[59] This fact, considered together with that of the Chenesi's great authority, discloses the religious basis of the confederacy.

Casañas and Massanet convey the impression that the Che-

[57] Alonso de León, Diario, 1689, AGN, Historia, vol. 27, fol. 18.
[58] Casañas, Relación, fols. 24–26; Espinosa, *Chrónica*, p. 424.
[59] Casañas, Relación, fol. 8.

nesi was a person of severe dignity, doing no manual labor and commanding great personal respect. He was fed and clothed by the community through gifts, to insure which he evidently sometimes preyed upon the superstitions of his people. He seldom left his lodge except to take exercise, attend ceremonials, and to visit. At the house of each of the caddis and "the most noble," a special seat of honor and a bed were scrupulously reserved for the use of the Chenesi during these visits. No one else dared sit in the Chenesi's seat for fear of supernatural death.[60] The caddis of the tribes made presents to the Chenesi, and when he died the most elaborate funeral ceremonials were performed.

The Head Civil Chief

Since in the Spanish reports native intertribal arrangements are confused with arrangements imposed on the Indians by the Spaniards, it is not always an easy matter to distinguish them; but it is clear, that as the Hainai was considered the head tribe, so was its caddi considered superior in rank and dignity to the other tribal chiefs. The Spaniards called him "*capitán grande.*"[61] The exact nature of his authority does not

[60] Massanet "Carta," p. 304.

[61] This point is so important and was so difficult to determine that it devolves on me to present some of the evidence. In 1716, Ramón spoke of a "*capitán grande*" in an ambiguous meaning but was apparently meaning a native head chief, as distinguished from the "*capitán general*" whom he ordered chosen by the Indians and upon whom he bestowed the *bastón*. Domingo Ramón, "Derrotero," AGN, Historia, vol. 27, fol. 157. In the same year, Espinosa tells us, the "Capitán General de los Indios Texas" fell sick. This man was very old and very much esteemed by all the people, while the man to whom Ramón gave the *bastón*, was young ("mozo Menor del capitán grande"). Hence the two could not have been the same, and the old man was evidently the native "head chief." Espinosa, *Chrónica*, p. 440. In 1721, Aguayo met at the Trinity River the cacique of the Hainai tribe, "whom all the Tribe tribes regard as superior" (the copy of Peña's Diario in Historia reads "Adays," but it is clear from the context that Hasinai is meant. Peña, Diario, fols. 34–41. Since the Spaniards had not been in the

appear. We know that, to the main village of his tribe came the Kadohadachos and other allies to make or renew their promises of friendship. Here the most important general councils were held, and over them the Hainai caddi perhaps presided.

A consideration that strengthens confidence in the general correctness of the foregoing view of the political organization of the Hasinai group is the fact that a close parallel is found in the organization of the Kadohadacho group on the Red River. They had a Great Chenesi, the Kadohadacho caddi was regarded as the head chief, and near his village was the group sanctuary, the famous hill of Zacado upon which the temple stood.[62]

Shamans and Medicine Men

The performance of religious and ceremonial rites was specialized, to a large extent, in the hands of the priestly, or shaman, class. The Chenesi was the high priest of the whole confederacy. The caddis, or civil chiefs, combined priestly with magisterial functions, and below them were numerous shamans of lesser rank. Solís regarded the tammas as priests, but evidently they were mainly administrative functionaries.[63] Within this

country for many months, this superiority of the Hainais could hardly have been due to an appointment by the Spaniards. While at the Hainai village where many chiefs were assembled, Peña called Cheocas, the chief of the Hainai village, "el Capitán Governador de todos los Texas" and referred to his great following; ibid., fols. 41–42. In 1727, Pedro Rivera spoke of the Hasinai tribe as "los Synays, Nación Capital de la Provincia de Thexas." Macarty's letter cited above was written in response to a claim by the governor of Texas that the "Hasinais" were the head tribe of all the Caddos. The French commandant made a counterclaim of that honor for the Kadohadachos, the fact being that the Hainais and the Kadohadoches were each head of a separate group.

[62] Terán, Diario, fols. 54–56; Macarty to Martos y Navarrete, November 17, 1763.

[63] Solís, Diario, fols. 248–97.

priestly class there was still further specialization of functions, some performing funeral rites, others war ceremonies, and so on. One specific illustration of this specialization is recorded in Espinosa's account of a functionary whose special business it was to repel the storms by conjuration, pray for rain, and be the first to bless a new crop.[64] Judging from Solís's report of Senate Adiva, a woman at the Nabedache village, and a statement made by Espinosa, women as well as men entered the priesthood and might attain high rank.[65]

Distinct from the priests, or shamans, but apparently with overlapping functions, there was a large class of medicine men known as *conna*. They had special insignia of office, in the form of peculiar headdresses, or curious necklaces of highly colored snake skins and other articles. They are also said always to have carried bow and arrows. At the houses, special seats were reserved for them, as for the chiefs and the priests.[66] To become a regularly qualified medicine man one had to go through an initiation, conducted by the priests and medicine men and lasting eight days. One part of this ceremony consisted of the candidate's drinking a stupefying concoction and, when he recovered, relating to the assembly his dreams or visions, like the minions of the old man of the mountain told by Marco Polo.[67]

Women and Children in the Social Organization

The traditional impression that the women were the burden-bearers of Indian society was acquired by the early observers with respect to the Hasinais. The servile lot which Casañas conceived to be theirs is reflected in his report that one of the prayers of the men was that they might have many women to

[64]Espinosa, *Chrónica*, p. 431.
[65]Ibid., p. 423.
[66]Ibid., pp. 427–29.
[67]Ibid., p. 429.

serve them.[68] Yet there was a more or less equitable division of labor in their economic life. The Spanish priests, who were more familiar with the domestic tasks of the women than with the labors of the men, were naturally more impressed with the burdensomeness of the former, and this may account in part for the somewhat distorted picture they give. An indication of the respectable position of women in Hasinai society, and a partial counter to the idea of complete servility, is the extensive part they took in many of the public ceremonials.

Marriage

One would scarcely in a society like that of the Hasinais expect to find matrimony on a very high plane, judged by civilized standards. "The marriage bond," says Espinosa, "is not solemnized with special ceremonies. However, the wills of the parents or brothers of the maiden are influenced by [the suitor's] carrying to them a stag or deer and leaving [it] for them at the door of the house, without speaking another word. If they take it inside and eat it, it is a sure sign that they give their consent. It is not necessary to await the will of the maiden for this is merged in the wish of her parents. "Thereupon they unite," as Father Acosta says of the people of Peru, "after the manner of animals." According to Casañas, in case the bride to be were a maiden, the caddi must be notified after the consent of the relatives was obtained, but if she were not a maiden only her consent, to be obtained by presents, was necessary.[69]

Monogamy was the rule, although polygamy was allowed and apparently existed to some extent. Casañas remarks, "What I praise is the fact that they never have more than one [wife] or if they do have another they do not regard her in the

[68] Casañas, Relación, fol. 8; Espinosa, Chrónica, p. 436; Margry, ed. and trans., Découvertes, 3:363.
[69] Espinosa, Chrónica, p. 427; Casañas, Relación, fol. 10.

same light as the first, living with both." Again, he tells us that the caddis ordinarily have only one wife, and that the wives of all the caddis are called by the common name Awuidau.[70] On the other hand, one remarkable case of polyandry was reported among the Hasinais by Solís in 1768, when he recorded in his diary the statement that at the Nabedache village there was a priestess or chieftianess who had five husbands.[71]

One reason for the exceptional character of polygamy was doubtless the looseness of the marriage tie. Our principal informant tells us that among the common people the relation continued ordinarily for only a few days, and rarely for life, because the women were easily allured to new mates by presents. Few men, he said, failed to separate from their first wife. Delisle, speaking of the Kadohadachos, said that the women changed spouses for slight causes, and as a consequence did not name their children after their husbands. Casañas observed no punishment for separation except the anger of the injured party, which caused no more serious trouble than a domestic quarrel. Neither did he observe any effort to conceal a breach of conjugal faith. Espinosa's version of the matter tallies with the others. "Among these people," he says,

matrimony endures as long as the wills are not unfavorable; then both seek other consorts . . . As to fidelity, some make a fuss if they are injured in this respect and punish their wives with blows; others either pay no attention to it, or *se hacen de la vista gorda,* for ordinarily among the Indians there is little redress in case their wives maintain *llanezas* and *juegas* with others of the same tribe.

Among the higher classes, Casañas thought, there was greater constancy, and he explained it by the fact that there were few with the temerity to disturb a dignitary in the peaceful possession of his wife.[72]

[70]Casañas, Relación, fol. 8.
[71]Solís, Diario, fol. 281.
[72]Casañas, Relación, fols. 9–10; Margry, ed. and trans., *Découvertes,* 3: 413; Espinosa, *Chrónica,* p. 427.

A practice that reflects Hasinai notions of marriage not un-common among the Indians of North America was that of the host offering his guest a mate during his stay.[73] On the other hand, Casañas's report, echoed later by other friars, [says] that the Hasinais, after a year's experience with unmarried sol-diers, protested against any more Spaniards coming without their families, indicates on the Indians' part a rather more jealous regard for their women than would seem consistent with his account of their marriage customs.[74]

Such marriage practices as the above were not indicative of or even compatible with a high degree of chastity among the women. In Casañas' opinion, those with the merest particle of honor were very few, while Joutel remarked that, although they showed no lewdness in public, they could be easily won by small presents.[75] Speaking generally of the relations be-tween the sexes, Espinosa said, "no notice is taken if they talk with each other with complete liberty, with jokes and pro-vocative witticisms; rather, they regard it as they would regard very witty jests. From this may be inferred the gross obscenity in which they are submerged."[76]

Childbirth and Childhood

A custom observed among the Kadohadocho and probably existing among the Hasinais, since it was quite widespread among the American Indians, was for the women to live sepa-rately during their periodical sickness. Says Delisle, "they have no commerce with the world, the people not even wish-ing that anyone should use their fire."[77] In regard to childbirth

[73] Margry, ed. and trans., *Découvertes*, 3: 355.
[74] Casañas, Relación, fol. 14.
[75] Ibid., fol. 10; Margry, ed. and trans., *Découvertes*, 3: 363.
[76] Espinosa, *Chrónica*, p. 427.
[77] Margry, ed. and trans., *Découvertes*, 3: 413; See J. Owen Dorsey, "Omaha Sociology," in *Third Annual Report* of the Bureau of American Eth-nology (1884), pp. 263, 267.

Solís reports: "the women effect parturition in the following manner: on the bank of the river or arroyo where they are settled they build little huts other than those they have to live in: in the middle they drive a stake, short, strong and very firm in the ground. When they feel the pains of childbirth coming on they go to these little huts and aiding themselves by these stakes they accomplish their labors. Then at once they go to the water, bathe themselves and the child, and come, with hair streaming, to the village where all the rest are. All this I have observed in this country." [78]

Our sources give us very little direct light on Hasinai child life, but a few things are reported, nevertheless. Soon after birth a child became the object of ceremonies suggesting to Espinosa that of christening. About the sixth or eighth day after the birth of a boy, according to this witness, a priest was called. Arriving at the house and sitting in a special seat, he took the child in his hands, fondled it, talked for a while in its ear, and then bathed it in a large vessel. Next he asked the parents what name was to be given it. "Ordinarily," says Espinosa "the one they designate is the diminutive of that of its parents." According to this, if both Joutel and Espinosa are correct, the Hasinai and the Kadohadacho customs in regard to naming children differed. The ceremony was concluded by a feast and giving presents to the priest. If the child were a girl a priestess performed the ceremony. [79]

Speaking of the Kadohadachos, Delisle said that they were very tender toward their children, adding "and the only way of chastising used by them is to throw water at them, without ever beating or giving ill words." [80] On the other hand, Casañas tells us that the Hasinai women practiced infanticide without attempt at concealment. In another instance he says that they were known to leave children to perish in a burning

[78] Solís, Diario, fol. 291.
[79] Espinosa, Chrónica, p. 427.
[80] Margry, ed. and trans., Découvertes, 3: 431; French, ed., Historical Collections, 1: 169.

house, saying that they were of no use.[81] This report, however, is not corroborated by that of other witnesses, which leads to the conclusion that such practices could not have been widespread. The high death rate from disease would also lead us to think that human life could not have been wasted prodigally.

If Espinosa can be trusted, children were early taught tribal religious rites, for he says, "even the little children, as soon as they show signs of reason, are so instructed in the errors of their elders as to cause me to wonder to hear them repeat all the rites and superstitions in which their parents had reared them." We know that boys were carefully trained in running and shooting, and it is presumably true that, as in other Indian societies, the children of both sexes were trained in the tasks their life duties would impose upon them.

---

[81] Casañas, Relación, fol. 10.

4

Economic Life

The Food Supply—Agriculture

A relatively large portion of the food supply of the Hasinais was obtained through agriculture. Their traditions did not go back to a time when they were not an agricultural people; indeed, they believed that their first ancestor, the revered Zacado, taught them to sow and to plant.[1] A Caddoan tradition still surviving among the reservation Indians tells that the Great Father gave the seed of all plants to Snake Woman, who distributed them to the rest of the world.[2] The description given above of the scattered villages affords an idea of the general nature of the agriculture settlements. It now remains to indicate the chief food-raising activities and to describe their means and methods of exploiting the soil.

Maize

Among the crops raised there were maize, beans, calabashes, sunflowers, tobacco, muskmelons (*melones*), and watermelons (*sandías*).[3] Maize, beans, and sunflowers were the staple food

[1] Chavalier Barthélemy de Macarty to Governor Ángel de Martos y Navarrete, Natchitoches, November 17, 1763, Nacogdoches Archives, Austin, Texas. A transcript is in the Bolton Papers, Bancroft Library. Fray Juan Agustín de Morfí uses this document but changes Zacado to Zacudo.

[2] George Amos Dorsey, *Traditions of the Caddo*, p. 18.

[3] Pierre Margry, ed. and trans., *Découvertes et établissements des français dans l' ouest et dans le sud de l'Amérique septentrionale, 1614–1754*, 3: 339, 342, 346, 394; Fry Francisco de Jesús María Casañas, "Relación," August 15,

crops, but among them all maize was by far the most important. Of this cereal they had two varieties, planted and harvested at different seasons. The early maize, according to Casañas, matured in six weeks; but according to Espinosa it was planted at the end of April and was ready for use at the end of May. This is incredible, and the other statement more convincing. The planting season was no doubt usually earlier than the end of April. The early variety of maize did not grow more than a yard high, a witness tells us, but produced many small and well-filled ears.[4] The larger variety, which constituted what the Indians called their "big sowing," matured in three months, according to Casañas, and in a shorter time, according to Espinosa. These two crops were sometimes raised on the same piece of land, the second being planted as soon as the ground could be cleared after the first had been harvested. Solís speaking of the Nabedache village, said they raised much corn, two crops a year, and three ears on every stalk. The size of these maize fields was frequently spoken of as considerable.[5]

Beans

Of beans Casañas reported five or six kinds, all very good. Joutel usually referred to them as "*fèves de Brazil.*" This fact might furnish botanists a clue to the varieties cultivated. It would seem that they were usually of the climbing sort, for we

1691, AGN, Historia, vol. 394, fol. 3; Damián Massanet, "Carta de Don Damian Mazanet a Don Carlos de Siguenza y Góngora Sobre el Descumbrimiento de la Bahia de Espiritu Santo," trans. Lilia M. Casis, *Quarterly* of the Texas State Historical Association 2 (April, 1899): 306; Domingo Ramón, "Derrotero," 1716, AGN, Historia, vol. 27, fols. 156, 158; Juan de la Peña, Diario, 1721–22, AGN, Historia, vol. 28, fol. 36; Isidro Felix de Espinosa, *Chrónica apostólica y seráphica de todos los colegios de propaganda fide de esta Nueva-España*, pp. 419, 421, 422.

[4]Casañas, Relación, fol. 3; Espinosa, *Chrónica*, pp. 421–22. Joutel was fed on green corn at the Nasoni village about June 1, 1687. See Margry, ed. and trans., *Découvertes*, 3: 392.

[5]Casañas, Relación, fol. 3; Espinosa, *Chrónica*, pp. 421–22; Fray Gaspar José de Solís, Diario." 1767, AGN, Historia, vol. 27, fol. 280.

are told that at each hill a cane or reed was stuck in the ground to enable the plant to climb and be free from water and vermin. When the ripened crop was harvested the cane and vine were pulled up together and carried to the house.[6]

Sunflowers

All the early observers mention the sunflower seed as an important article of consumption and the culture of the sunflower as one of the regular activities among these people. The sunflowers were reported as "very large," which, of course, is an indefinite term.[7] They mixed ground sunflower seeds with cornmeal and made nutritious cakes or tamales.

Tobacco

Tobacco, which though not a food crop, was regularly cultivated and should therefore be mentioned here, seems to have been plentiful. Ramón says that of it "they have much," and Espinosa tells us that "they never fail to produce it in season." Joutel said that it was of a sort having smaller leaves than French tobacco and almost evergreen. They powdered the dried leaves of the plant, carried it in little sacks for smoking, and used it freely in their religious and social ceremonials.[8]

---

[6]Casañas, Relación, fol. 3; Margry, ed. and trans., Découvertes, 3: 343; Espinosa, Chrónica, p. 422. La Harpe reported that the Nassonites on the Red River raised three kinds of beans. Margry, ed. and trans., Découvertes, 6: 264.

[7]Espinosa, Chrónica, p. 419; Margry, ed. and trans., Découvertes, 3:343, 346; Casañas, Relación, fol. 3. Among the products of the Hasinais, Ramón (1716) enumerates "maize, sandias, trixoles, tavaco, y una flour anteada que tienen ellas, que comen mui buen de ella, quo no le sabemos el nombre." Ramón, "Derrotero," fol. 158. Does he refer to the plant like the "col" mentioned by Casañas (see below) or to the sunflower?

[8]Benjamin F. French, ed., Historical Collections of Louisiana, 2:151; Ramón, "Derrotero," 1716, fol. 155; Massanet, "Carta," p. 302; Espinosa, Chrónica, p. 431.

Minnie Parton and Charley Parton, Caddo Indians. Photograph by James Mooney in 1893 in Oklahoma. Courtesy National Anthropological Archives (neg. no. 1371-A), Smithsonian Institution.

Other Crops

Casañas tells us, after enumerating maize, beans, calabashes, watermelons, and sunflowers, that "among the grains that they sow in season" there is "another grain like the seed of *coles*," of which, ground with maize, they make powder (*polvos*), to eat which it is necessary to have water near by, since it is like flour, and if eaten dry it sticks in the throat."[9] I have not been able to identify this plant.

In addition to the above-cultivated crops, Morfí (c.1782) tells of "very fine orchards" of peach, cherry, fig, hazelnut, chestnut, medlar, pomegranate, strawberry, and other fruits. He also tells about the Hasinais breeding chickens and turkeys for profit. This statement seems open to question. If anyone was in a position to know these facts it was Espinosa, but, although his catalogue of wild fruits in the Hasinai country corresponds closely with Morfí's above list of "orchard" products, he says nothing about cultivated fruits nor of domesticated chickens and turkeys. Neither does Mézières, who in the later eighteenth century described the agriculture of some of these Indians. Morfí apparently read Espinosa's list of wild fruits and nuts and supposed they grew in orchards.[10]

Methods of Cultivation

The methods of cultivation practiced were of course rudimentary. In preparing the ground the brush and weeds were cleared off and the soil lightly scratched with a crude instrument, the usual one being a mattox, or pick, made of bone or of fire-hardened wood tied by bark cord to a wooden handle.

[9] Casañas, Relación, fol. 3.

[10] Juan Agustin Morfí, "Historia de Texas," trans. F. F. Hilder, MS 1750 in the National Anthropological Archives, Smithsonian Institution, bk. 3, p. 102; Athanase de Mézières, "Informe," 1772, British Museum, Add. MS 17574, fol. 2, and Add. MS 17567, fol. 17; De Mézières to Teodoro de Crois, Pueblo de los Quitseis, August 30, 1779, AGN, Provincias Internas, vol. 182, fol. 48; also in Historia, vol. 28, fol. 242.

The favorite wood used for this purpose was walnut (*nogal*), and we may suppose that, as was the case with the neighboring Plains Indian, the favorite bone was the shoulder blade of the buffalo. At the coming of the Europeans the Hasinais had no iron tools. It has already been stated that after the first crop of small corn was removed, the ground was again cleaned and a second crop of the larger variety of corn was planted. No mention of the use of fertilizers appears in the sources.[11]

Although the products of the fields seem to have been family property,[12] the ground was prepared for the seed and the seed sown by community labor. All the early observers including Joutel, Casañas, and Espinosa, mention this feature of Hasinai economic life. When it was time to plant, the men and women of a whole village, "sometimes more than a hundred persons," including the caddi, assembled to prepare the fields, family by family, taken in order according to the rank of men in the councils. If we may judge from Espinosa's statement about the community building of houses, we may suppose that the caddis only supervised the work of clearing.[13] We are told that before the house of the Gran Chenesi only a little patch was sown, and this was not for consumption, since he was fed by the community, but "that he might have something green for his recreation."[14] Work continued until noon, the rest of the day being spent in eating and sports. Thus the occasion had a social as well as an economic significance.[15] In order that there might be someone to prepare the feast, the household whose ground was being planted was exempt from work in the field.[16] It was like "bee work" in a frontier Ameri-

[11] Margry, ed. and trans., *Découvertes*, 3: 364; Espinosa, *Chrónica*, p. 421. Espinosa says that the ground was cleared (*impiada*) and scratched to a depth of a *quarta*. Morfí, "Historia de Texas," bk. 3, renders *quarta* as "a few inches."

[12] Margry, ed. and trans., *Découvertes*, 3: 363–64.

[13] Ibid.; Espinosa, *Chrónica*, p. 421; Casañas, Relación, fol. 8.

[14] Casañas, Relación, fol. 9.

[15] Margry, ed. and trans., *Découvertes*, 3: 363; Espinosa, *Chrónica*, p. 421.

[16] Note the same custom in connection with community buildings, below.

can community. In this planting, there was a differentation of tasks on the basis of sex. The men aided only in clearing and stirring the soil, leaving the planting to the women. This may explain why the men and women worked in separate groups. No pregnant woman was allowed to assist at the sowing for fear, through some superstition, that the crops would be spoiled, hence most of this work as well as the subsequent care of the fields was left to old women.[17] The sowing season, like the harvest, the building, and the hunting seasons, were attended by extensive religious ceremonials.[18]

When the maize was harvested, such of it as was not eaten green was either shelled and preserved in large vessels in the houses, or stored in the ear by being placed on pole platforms or hung in braised strings on forked posts. The best ears were carefully preserved in this way for seed.[19] To keep insects out of the baskets of shelled maize and beans, the tops were sprinkled with ashes.[20]

Espinosa tells us that the Hasinais always saved seed corn enough for two years, so that if the first year's harvest should fail they would still have seed for the second. This supply was so carefully guarded, he said, that even though the food supply of corn should be exhausted the seed was not touched.[21]

Preagricultural Activities

Besides the foods derived from cultivated crops, the Hasinais consumed products furnished more directly by nature in the form of wild plants, game, and fish. Among the more substantial wild vegetable foods used by them were nuts, acorns, and the tuqui, or toque root. Espinosa says they gathered for the year's supply a large quantity of acorns and of walnuts (*nogales*)

---

[17]Casañas, Relación, fol. 1; Margry, *Découvertes*, 3: 364; Espinosa, *Chrónica*, p. 421.

[18]French, ed., *Historical Collections*, 1: 515.

[19]Espinosa, *Chrónica*, p. 422.

[20]Ibid.

[21]Ibid.

of two kinds, one large and hard, and the other small and soft.[22] The supply was gathered in the fall and winter by the women, who stored it in the houses in baskets and jars as they did the shelled maize.[23]

Among the other products that abounded in the forest, and which we are led to infer the Hasinais ate, were the medlar [a fruit resembling a crab apple], chestnuts with fruit "like the acorn," mulberries, blackberries, plums, "asses," and pomegranates "like those in China."[24] "Wild olives" were boiled and used for a drink, at least in the ceremonials.[25]

A root that was much used was the "tuqui," "tuque," or "toquo."[26] Douay described its use[27] in 1686, in a way that may help to identify the plant. "They served it to us," he said, "among other things, a porridge (sagamite) made of a kind of root called toque, or toquo. It is a shrub, like a kind of bramble without thorns, and has a very large root, which they wash perfectly, after which it is pounded and reduced to powder in a mortar. The sagamity has a good taste, though astringent."[28] Solís (1768), referring to its use among the Hasinais, calls it "tuqui," and says it "is like the casava of Havana, since it is from the roots of a certain tree."[29] Solís is authority for the statement that this root was eaten with bear's

[22] "Nogales muy gruessons, que dan la nuez encarcelada: y otra especie de Nogales de Nuez pequena, y mollar, de que se abastecen los Indios," ibid., p. 419.

[23] Ibid., p. 436; Massanet, "Carta," pp. 304–305.

[24] Casañas, Relación, fols. 2, 3; Espinosa, Chrónica, p. 419; Massanet, "Carta," pp. 304–305. Joutel also tells of the use of vessels to contain fruits.

[25] Espinosa, Chrónica, p. 432.

[26] French, ed., Historical Collections, 4: 199, calls it toque or toquo; Solís, "Diario," fol. 280, calls it tuqui. Espinosa apparently does not mention it.

[27] Among the Biskatronges between the Colorado and the Brazos.

[28] French, ed., Historical Collections, 4: 199. For the meaning of sagamite see Frederick W. Hodge, ed., Handbook of the American Indians North of Mexico Bureau of American Ethnology Bulletin 30 (1910), 2: 407–408.

[29] Morfí says they mixed it with bear's grease "and nothing else," but this seems to be a misreading of Solís, whom he was following at his point. Fray Gaspár José de Solís, Diario, 1767, AGN, Historia, vol. 27, fol. 280; Fray Juan Agustín Morfí, "Historia," trans. Hilder, 3: 102.

fat.[30] Casañas may have been referring to the same plant when, enumerating the wild foods afforded the Hasinai Indians, he said, "there are roots like yams [batatas] which grow in the ground, and are very good."[31] Since Casañas said the root was *like* "the yam," which he doubtless knew, we can hardly suppose it was the yam.

When the maize crop was bad, they used as a substitute for it in making their cakes (*poleadas*) the seed of hollow reed grass (*carrizo, que más es otatillo hueco*). The seed was like grains of wheat and was roasted before using.[32] This description suggests wild rice.

Hunting and Fishing—Small Game and Fish

Although for buffalo and bear the Hasinais had to go some distance, small game and fish were plentiful in the lake and timber country they occupied. Some Indians of the Caddoan stock were said not to eat fish,[33] but we are told that the Hasinais made free use of the piscatorial supply in the rivers and lakes near by.[34] In the immediate neighborhood there was an abundance of wild hogs (*jalotes*) "very fat and good," wild cats (*gatos montezes*), badgers (*tejones*), deer, rabbits, wild turkey, partridges, quail, heron, and, in season, ducks of various kinds. The Indians apparently used all of these for food.[35]

Buffalo

To the Plains Indian the buffalo was the primary means of subsistence. Besides furnishing the staple food, it provided a

[30] Solís, Diario, fol. 280.

[31] Casañas, Relación, fol. 3.

[32] Espinosa, *Chrónica*, p. 422.

[33] Mézières's description of the Taovayas or Wichita; De Mézières to Croix, April 18, 1778, AGN, Provincias Internas, vol. 182, fol. 29; AGN, Historia, vol. 28, fol. 276.

[34] Espinosa, *Chrónica*, p. 422.

[35] Ibid., p. 429; Casañas Relación, fol. 3.

variety of other essential commodities. The brains were used for softening leather, the skull for ladles and drinking vessels, the shoulder blades for hoes or picks for cultivating the soil, small bones for awls, the tendons for bowstrings, the hoofs for glue to attach the arrow-tails, the tail-hair to make ropes and belts, the droppings for fuel, the hide to provide bridle, saddle and tether ropes for the horses, as well as to furnish shields, tents, traveling bags, footwear, beds and blankets, and coffins for the Indians, a surprising array of gifts from one clumsy, ugly beast.[36]

As the Hasinais were an agricultural people who had come, it is believed by some, from the southeast to the borders of the prairies, and had only within comparatively recent times hunted the buffalo,[37] this animal was not so all-important to them as to the semiplains and plains Indians in the west and north. Yet even to the Hasinais it was very important as a means of supplying meat, clothing, and various utensils; while for ceremonial purposes the fat of buffalo heart was highly prized. Accordingly, at different times of the year, but more usually in winter, when the buffalo was ranging south in greater numbers, when the cows were fat, and when the vegetable food supply was getting low, parties were organized to go to the prairies in search of this ponderous animal.[38]

The nearest good ground for hunting buffalo was some four

[36]Mézières to Croix, San Xavier River, September 22, 1779, AGN, Provincias Internas, vol. 182, fol. 58, which refers to the Tonkawa Indians west of the middle Brazos; see Mrs. Edward E. Ayer, trans., "Benavides's Memorial, 1630," *Land of Sunshine* 14 (1901): 43–44, for an early summary in the "Relación Posteera de Sivola," cited by Hodge, ed., *Handbook* 1: 169–70. Editor's note: For an in-depth study see Tom McHugh, *The Time of the Buffalo* (New York, 1972), pp. 83–109.

[37]Dorsey, *Traditions*, p. 5.

[38]Casañas, Relación, fol. 3; Massanet, "Carta," p. 306; Espinosa, *Chrónica*, p. 422. Arriciorta says the Apaches hunted twice a year, particularly in December and January, when the cows were fat and they went north to hunt. In May and June they returned to kill the bulls; Espinosa, *Chrónica*, , p. 391; see also Hodge, ed., *Handbook* 1: 169–70.

days' journey west of the Neches.[39] At the coming of the French these animals did not range, in the latitude of the Hasinais, much east of the Brazos and Navasota rivers. La Salle's party, in February and March, 1687, found them in plenty all the way from the mouth of the La Vaca River northeastward to the Brazos, but east of that river there were few.[40] Joutel specifically states that beyond the place where La Salle was murdered, only a short distance from the Brazos, there were none.[41] La Salle had noted the same thing in 1686 and his reason for hiding food near the Brazos on his way back to Fort St. Louis was to provide against scarcity when he should recross the country between the Brazos, where the buffalo supply ended, and the Hasinai country, where corn could be had.

This was the experience of Massanet in July, 1691, who crossed the Brazos higher up than did La Salle's party. He mentioned buffalo all the way from a point south of the Rio Grande to the Navasota River, but none beyond that stream.[42] It would thus seem that the Brazos and the Navasota formed the buffalo line.

[39] Casañas, Relación, fol. 3. Espinosa says that it was more than forty leagues to the buffalo grounds. His point of reference was the Hasinai village on the Angelina River. Espinosa, Chrónica, , p. 422.

[40] Margry, ed. and trans., Découvertes, 3: 150, 151, 158, 167, 214, 263–65, 269–71. They were more plentiful south of the Colorado River than north of it. Ibid., pp. 293, 302, 308. For a map of the buffalo range in Texas see Brownie Ponton and Bates H. M'Farland, "Álvar Nuñez Cabeza de Vaca: A Preliminary Report on His Wanderings in Texas," Quarterly of the Texas State Historical Association 1 (January, 1898): 176.

[41] Margry, ed. and trans., Découvertes, 3: 336. Mention was made of killing only two animals east of the Brazos River, and these were taken the day of La Salle's death. Ibid., pp. 319–20.

[42] Douay, Diary, May 16–August 2, 1687. It will be noted that these expeditions were made at different times of the year. La Salle returned to Fort St. Louis in 1686 in the middle of October. French, ed., Historical Collections, 4: 206. The expedition that Joutel accompanied crossed the Brazos in the middle of March; Margry, ed. and trans., Découvertes, 3: 317. Massanet's expedition crossed near the end of July; Diario, 1691, AGN, Historia, vol. 27, fol. 108.

The prime hunting ground in the latitude of the Hasinais was between the Brazos and San Antonio rivers, and to this field Indians came a long distance every year, from the east and from the west.[43] Both La Salle in 1687 and Massanet in 1690 met Hasinai Indians hunting between the Brazos and the Colorado.[44] From the Brazos to the Trinity they had a well-beaten path leading from their villages to the hunting grounds. This trail Joutel's party followed to the Nabedache town after the death of La Salle.[45] This highway apparently became later a part of the famous Camino Real or San Antonio Road.

Bear

Next to the buffalo, the bear was most important among the game hunted at a distance. It was plentiful in the north, but was not ordinarily found in the neighborhood of the Hasinai settlements. Only once during the several years spent by Espinosa among these Indians were live bears seen by him in the neighborhood of Mission Concepción. This was in the very severe winter of 1722, when bears were driven to the settlements by hunger.[46] From these bear hunts great quantities of fat were brought home rolled up in moss (*heno*). We are told that in later years the French obtained 2,000 barrels of bear's fat a year in trade among the east Texas tribes.[47] After it was "tried out," the lard was preserved in vessels, to be used in various ways during the year. The natives were very fond of this product, even using it melted as a drink. To it the Spaniards attributed much of the sickness among the Indians, par-

[43]Near the site of New Braunfels, Massanet's party encountered a ranchería of two or three thousand Indians, largely members of tribes from the west. Among them were the Jumanos of New Mexico and Parrál, who came every year to the Guadalupe River to hunt. Massanet, Diario, 1691, AGN, Historia, vol. 27, fol. 100.

[44]Margry, ed. and trans., *Découvertes*, 3: 311; Massanet, "Carta," p. 300.

[45]Margry, ed. and trans., *Découvertes*, 3: 325, 332.

[46]Espinosa, *Chrónica*, p. 422.

[47]See Solís, Diario, 1767, AGN, Historia, vol. 27, fol. 280; Espinosa, *Chrónica*, p. 422.

ticularly dysentery. The skins of the bear were also a valuable product and were used for various purposes.

Means and Methods of Hunting

The chief weapons used by the Hasinais for hunting were the bow and arrow.[48] In hunting deer and turkeys and perhaps buffalo as well, they used disguises. To deceive the deer they would place on their heads a deer's antlers and paint their bodies or throw skins over themselves. For hunting the turkey, covers of feathers were used.[49] Morfí (ca. 1782) reported that for hunting purposes "they breed a particular species of dogs that they call '*tubines*,' large-boned and active, and as cunning as their masters."[50] I do not know the sources of this statement; therefore, I withhold full credence. Certain it is that the Hasinais had dogs and took them along on their buffalo-hunting trips, but as for their use of them as aids in hunting I have only Morfi's word, which is not always the best.

Before starting on a deer hunt, the Hasinais performed a peculiar ceremonial. A dried deer's head, with neck and antlers attached, was set up on the house, and a petition was made to the Caddi Ayo that he would deliver the deer [as] a prize into the hunter's hands. During the pauses in the ceremony, which lasted an hour, we are told, the Indians smoked powdered tobacco. The ceremony over, they placed the deer's head at the lodge door; then, painting his naked body with white earth, or covering it with skins, and using a similar deer's head for a decoy, the hunter set forth. When a deer was killed the hunter would talk to it awhile in the ear before bringing it in. Says Espinosa, "they observe the custom that he who kills [the deer] does not eat it unless another invites him, or unless he has no other way to satisfy his hunger."[51]

[48] Casañas, Relación, fol. 3.

[49] Espinosa, Chrónica, p. 431.

[50] Morfí, "Historia," trans. Hilder, 3: 103.

[51] Espinosa, Chrónica, p. 431. Note that in some tribes the person who killed the buffalo had a specially fine portion of the meat.

Little Boy, also known as George Washington Caddo-Hasinai leader in Oklahoma. During the Civil War he served in the Confederate army as captain of a company of Indian scouts. Photographed by Alexander Gardner, Washington D.C., 1872. Courtesy National Anthropological Archives (neg. no. 1366-A), Smithsonian Institution.

The Hasinais generally hunted buffalo in large parties, because most of their enemies were towards the west, and there were many chances of them meeting on the hunting grounds.[52] The starting of a buffalo hunting expedition was preceded by very elaborate religious ceremonies to ensure its success.[53] When the grounds were reached the party scattered out in smaller groups the better to find game.[54] Of rules governing the chase, such as other tribes observed, and these also perhaps, we get no knowledge from our sources. Horses were not very plentiful among the Hasinais at the coming of La Salle, and most of the hunting was done on foot, with bows and arrows, the Indians running the buffalo down, but horses, and no doubt dogs, were used to carry home the skins and meat.

Salt

As coming under the general head of food supply it may be said that salt was procured from the salt marshes that abounded in the northwestern part of the Hasinai territory.[55] It is probable that the Hasinais, like the Kadohadacho, made expeditions to the Grand Saline in Van Zandt County, for supplies for this commodity.

The Indian was limited to the seasons for variety in his food, and in consequence his diet at any given time was apt to

[52] Casañas, Relación, fols. 1–3; Espinosa, Chrónica, p. 422.

[53] Casañas, Relación, fol. 7.

[54] La Salle "told us that there were several bands of these people [the Hasinais] hunting in this country [between the Colorado and the Brazos] dispersed in various places, the better to subsist, as is their custom"; Margry, ed. and trans., Découvertes, 3: 311. Joutel learned about the same time that "there were fifty persons (hunters) in four or five cabins, and that their people were in several places in the vicinity"; ibid., p. 312. For the hunting rules of other tribes see Hodge, ed., Handbook, 1: 160–70.

[55] According to Joutel the "Naodiche" or "Nahordikhe" village was so named because of the salt nearby. From this place the Nasonis ("Assonis") procured salt. Margry, ed. and trans., Découvertes, 3: 387–88, 394. For the method of utilizing salt see below.

be a simple one. Corn and ground nuts came nearest to being continual staples. In the spring, before the early crop of corn was ready, string beans might constitute his whole menu for a week. Then would come the green corn season, then the summer fruits, later melons and squashes, then the ripe corn followed by nuts and acorns. The winter was the time for long fasts broken by great feasts on buffalo and bear's meat.

Preparation of Food

Foodstuffs thus procured by agriculture, by root-digging, fruit, nut, and seed-gathering, and by hunting was prepared in a variety of ways. One fact by no means unique but worthy of note, is that the major portion of the food seems to have been cooked before being consumed. Fruits were no doubt usually eaten raw, but other vegetable foods and meat were usually subjected to heat. In the communal house much of the cooking was done in common in large earthen pots over the central fire, and the resulting product was divided among the inmates by the head woman,[56] or *maîtresse de femmes*. The most instructive method of discussing home cookery, perhaps, will be to take the preparation of the different food substances separately.

Meat, according to Casañas, was never eaten raw, but always either roasted or boiled and without broth.[57] It is hard to say whether roasting or boiling was more prevalent, for both were much used. Joutel tells of eating smoked meat (*boucanée*) among the Nasonis; and the custom of smoking it that was early observed even among the Karankawa, was probably practiced among all the Hasinais, for they hunted buffalo and bear far from home and had to cure their meat to preserve it.[58] One method of curing it mentioned by Espinosa among the

[56] Ibid., 3: 393.
[57] "De la carne nunca hazen mas que dos quizados cocido y azado . . . y due como comen siempre la carne cocido y assado sin caldo," Casañas, Relación, fol. 4.
[58] Margry, ed. and trans., *Découvertes*, 3: 389.

Hasinais was simply to dry it.[59] The process was probably that of "jerking" i.e., cutting the meat in long thin strips and drying it in the sun.[60] This method was widespread among the natives.

A large portion of the maize, the standard food article, was roasted and consumed when green,[61] but the ripened maize and other grains, as well as nuts and roots, were ordinarily ground into flour before being cooked. The maize, as a rule, was parched on the coals previous to grinding.[62]

The grinding was effected by wooden mortars, the process being thus described: "The women parch the maize and then grind it into very fine flour. If the savages had mills it would much lighten their work, for this is a great task.[63] They have large mortars they make from the trunk of a tree, hollowed out with fire to a certain depth, after which they scrape and shape it. As many as four women grind the corn. Each one has a large pestle nearly five feet long, and they keep time like blacksmiths when they strike upon their anvil. When they have ground a certain time they take out the flour, and other women pass it through little sieves that they make very well of large reeds. When they wish to have the flour very fine they shake it upon small flat baskets (*vanettes*). The finest flour remains attached to the bottom, and coarser and the bran coming to the top. In this way they make it as fine as possible, indeed, as fine as I have seen it in France or elsewhere."[64] In

[59] Espinosa, *Chrónica*, p. 429.

[60] Mézières, in 1772, speaking of the Kichai ("Quitseis"), neighbors of the Hasinais, with very similar habits, writes: ". . . they have the same custom of absenting themselves during the cold season for the purpose of getting a full supply of dried meat, which is kept for other seasons of the year." Mézières to Baron de Ripperdá, July 4, 1772, AGN, Provincias Internas, vol. 20, fol. 28.

[61] Margry, ed. and trans., *Découvertes*, 3: 400; Espinosa, *Chrónica*, p. 434.

[62] Margry, ed. and trans., *Découvertes*, 3: 340, 367.

[63] Solís, in 1768, tells of the high price of Mexican metates among the Hasinais. Diario, fol. 280.

[64] Margry, ed. and trans., *Découvertes*, 3: 367.

the house of the Nabedache chief (caddi) Massanet saw six or seven wooden mortars. These were used in rainy weather. In pleasant weather, the flour was ground outside in other mortars.[65] Very well made mortars were mentioned by Espinosa.[66]

The flour made by the Indians of parched maize the Spaniards called *pinole*.[67] According to Joutel it was usual among the Hasinais to eat this pinole without further cooking, "since it was already cooked."[68] When thus consumed it ws either mixed with water, as *atole*, or perhaps with bear's grease or broth, or eaten dry.[69] In spite of what Joutel says to the effect that pinole was usually eaten without further cooking, it seems that the flour was very commonly made into a boiled mush. It was also made into a sort of a boiled bread or pudding, and again, baked into a loaf on the coals. Joutel said that when hot these loaves were very good.[70] A loaf (*bolla*) or cake made of corn mixed with sunflower seed and called by the natives "*bojan*," Espinosa compared to *alfajor*. Sometimes a stew was made of corn flour and beans, "which is not, however," said Joutel, with the gustatory discrimination of his race, "a very good dish, but this is their way."[71] It seems that unground corn was sometimes stewed with beans.[72] It was also mixed with the seeds of the plant like "col," and served as a powder with water. If water were not used it caused choking.[73] It was customary to wrap in corn husks (*fouilles*) whatever was boiled.[74] This may be what led Casañas, de León, and Massanet to call certain dishes "tamales."

[65] Massanet, "Carta," p. 304.
[66] Espinosa, *Chrónica*, pp. 435–36.
[67] Massanet, "Carta," p. 302; Espinosa, *Chrónica*, p. 434.
[68] Margry, ed. and trans., *Découvertes*, 3: 340.
[69] Massanet, "Carta," p. 303; Espinosa, *Chrónica*, p. 431.
[70] Margry, ed. and trans., *Découvertes*, 3: 343, 346, 364; Espinosa, *Chrónica*, pp. 419, 432.
[71] Margry, ed. and trans., *Découvertes*, 3: 364.
[72] Massanet, "Carta," p. 394.
[73] Casañas, Relación, fol. 3.
[74] Margry, ed. and trans., *Découvertes*, 3: 364.

Beans were cooked green or ripe. Joutel's description of the way "string beans" were served to him at the Nasoni village is an illustration of the crude methods of cooking and of the way in which salt was procured and utilized for seasoning foods.

This it was that obliged me to take care of our good old lady, for she furnished us food. True, this consisted usually of nothing more than green beans, of which these savages grow a goodly quantity. . . . But they do not make a great mystery of preparing them. They merely put them into a large pot, without even removing the strings. Then they cover them with grapevine leaves until they are nearly cooked. There is a certain sand to obtain which they go toward the hamlet that we last found, which is called Naoudiche, meaning salt . . . of this sand they take a handful or two, more or less, according to what they have to salt, put it in water to soak awhile, and then pour the water on the beans or meat which they wish to salt. . . . This is the only seasoning that we had to flavor these beans with. When they were cooked the good old lady gave us each our portions on a bark platter.[75]

Of tuqui, Solís, writing in 1768, said that after grinding it they drank it with bear's fat, and that the consumption of bear's fat in this way was the cause of bloody dysentery, small-pox, and other troubles.[76] By the Biskatronges, far to the west, the toque was washed, dried, powdered in a mortar and served as a porridge (sagamite).[77] Nuts, acorns, sunflower seeds, and the seed of the plant like "*col*" were sometimes used separately to make bread or stews, but more commonly it seems, they were mixed with other and with maize flour to make the various dishes described.[78] Drinks, for ceremonial purposes at least, were made by boiling various herbs. One such was made out of what Espinosa called wild olives.

[75] Ibid., p. 394.
[76] Solís, Diario, fol. 280.
[77] French ed., *Historical Collections*, 4: 198.
[78] For acorns stewed in meat broth see Margry, ed and trans., *Découvertes*, 3: 389; for nut bread see ibid., p. 343; for a mixture of sunflower seed with corn to make tamales, see Casañas, Relación, fol. 3; for the use of seed "like col" see ibid.; for nut tamales see Massanet, "Carta," p. 304.

5

Housing, Hardware, Handicrafts

The Building Arts—Architecture

The character of the architecture of a given tribe or group of Indians depended upon several factors, such as their capacity, racial habits, and characteristics; their cultural and social status; the influence of neighboring cultures; the physiography of the district occupied, especially the building materials available; and finally, climate.[1] Some of these general influences are evident in Hasinai architecture. Thus we find their buildings of a permanent nature suited to their settled life, and their architecture shaped by climate conditions and the available building material of a timber and grass country. They belonged, architecturally considered, to the large class of grass lodge builders, including among others the Wichita group, and representing a middle grade of Indian culture. Their development was such that they were not content with dwellings alone, but extended their architectural efforts beyond mere habitations to the provision of special structures for civic, social, religious, and even agricultural purposes.

[1]Frederick Webb Hodge, ed., *Handbook of American Indians North of Mexico,* Bureau of American Ethnology Bulletin no. 30 (1907), 1: 77–82. Editor's note: For an in-depth study of Hasinai housing see Edwin N. Wilmsen, "A Suggested Developmental Sequence for House Forms in the Caddoan Area," *Bulletin* of the Texas Archaeological Society 30 (1959): 35–50.

Habitations

Of primary importance, of course, was house building. The substantial structure and the furnishings of the Hasinai houses were such as to strike the attention of one journeying eastward from the country of the Plains or Coast Indians, for the latter lived mainly in temporary tipis made of skins or reeds.[2] All early observers agree in the general description of the Hasinai houses. Joutel writes, "There are ordinarily eight or ten families in these cabins (*cabanas*), which are very large, for some of them are as much as sixty feet in diameter. They are made differently from those we have seen by the way (from Matagorda Bay). They are round, in the form of beehives, or better, like large haycocks, having the same form except that they are higher. They are covered with grass from bottom to top. They make the fire in the middle, the smoke going out at the top through the grass." To make the houses "they cut tall trees as thick through as a man's thigh. These they set in the ground in a circle and join them at the top; then they lath (*lattent*) them and cover them from the top to the bottom."[3] Douay (1686) said the houses were forty or fifty feet high, each one holding two families.[4] On the other hand, French's edition of Joutel says there were sometimes fifteen or twenty families in each.[5] Massanet said that the house of the caddi of the Nabedache was twenty *varas* [Spanish measurement approximately 2 feet in length] high.[6] Joutel tells us that the dwellings

[2] Pierre Margry, ed. and trans., *Découvertes et établissements des français dans l'ouest et dans le sud de l'Amérique Septentrionale, 1614–1754*, 3: 297–98; Casañas, in Relación, reported that he heard that the Kadohadachos and the Natchitoches (Nasitox) built their houses closer together than the Hasinais, however, see La Harpe to the contrary.

[3] Ibid., 3: 345.

[4] Benjamin F. French, ed., *Historical Collections of Louisiana*, 4: 204.

[5] Ibid., 1: 148.

[6] Damián Massanet, "Carta de Don Damian Mazanet a Don Carlos de Siguenza y Góngora sobre el Descubrimiento de la Bahia de Espiritu Santo," trans. Lilia M. Casis, *Quarterly* of the Texas State Historical Association 2 (April, 1899): 303.

of the Nasonis, though not so high as those of the Cenis (Nabedaches and Neches) were made in the same way and like them accommodated several families.[7] There were no windows to these habitations and only one door.[8] The framework consisted of long rib-poles set in a circle. In the center a forked tree was set so that two men could mount it and tie the tops of the poles together, and when the house was finished the center pole was cut down. Crosswise laths were tied with strong bark cords. The covering was grass "longer than wheat straw," laid on like a thatch, beginning at the bottom. At the top of the house often there was some kind of fanciful crown likewise made of grass. The chief difference between individual houses as that those occupied by the caddi, the chenesi, and the principal men, were not only larger, but were also better made through having more rib-poles than the others.[9]

Community labor was observed in building houses as well as in preparing the fields. Espinosa tells us that when a man wished to build a dwelling he informed the caddi. This person ordered the tammas to run to all the houses of the settlement notifying the inhabitants to come and help at the building on a certain day. The messenger took as many little sticks in his hand as there were to be ribs in the house, leaving one or more at each house, as a signal that each recipient must cut a pole,[10] trim it, carry it to the appointed place, and set it in the

[7]Margry, ed. and trans., *Découvertes*, 3: 393–94. Mézières in 1779 reported that the Taovayas or Wichita houses, at their villages on the Red River, had an average of ten or twelve beds each; De Mézières to Croix; April 18, 1778, AGN, Historia, vol. 28, fol. 276. The party of thirty-eight men, women, and children taken by Mooney to the Omaha exposition in 1898 lived while there in a single grass lodge that they had taken to pieces on the reservation and set up again at Omaha. James Mooney to Herbert E. Bolton, January 13, 1907. Editor's note: This letter could not be found among the Bolton papers.

[8]Massanet, "Carta," p. 303.

[9]Isidro Felix de Espinosa, *Chrónica apostólica, y seráphica de todos los colegios de propaganda fide de este Nueva-España*, p. 420.

[10]Writing in 1726, Espinosa said that the *tammas* went about on horseback. This custom, of course, must have been of comparatively recent date,

hole assigned to him. Others were ordered to bring slender poles for the crosspieces or laths and bark thongs with which to tie them. One or two women from each house were ordered to carry each her bundle of long grass to use for covering. On the eve of the day of the building the tammas warned the people to be ready and went themselves to sleep at the place where the building was to be erected. Next day was a great occasion. At daybreak the caddi came and took his seat, not to work, but to direct things. At the signal given by the tammas each person appointed came running with his pole on his shoulder and deposited it in the awaiting hole.[11] Two men next mounted the center pole and tied the ribs together, then each one who had brought cross laths fastened them to the poles brought by his household. This task of lathing occupied about an hour. Then a new crew, composed mainly of women, put on the grass thatch, beginning at the bottom. Soon after midday the covering would be in place. Meanwhile the tammas went about with switches of green withes, enlivening the work by their presence or by blows.

These house buildings were in the nature of social gatherings, like cornhuskings or raisings on the Anglo-American frontier, and the more important the personage for whom the home was being made, the more sumptuous was the feast provided. As in the communal planting, the owners of the new house, instead of working, dispensed the supply of food previously provided. The building done and the feasting over, the assembly dispersed.[12]

The priests took an important part in the building of the houses, their function being to make the measurements and to perform the appropriate religious ceremonies.[13] Joutel tells us

---

though it was probably practiced at the coming of the Spaniards, for the Hasinais already had horses; ibid.

[11] Ibid.
[12] Ibid.
[13] Ibid., p. 428.

that when the Hasinais removed from one place to another they generally burned their dwellings.[14] Such were the grass lodges and the process of building them as described by early witnesses. Perhaps a careful study of the grass lodges built by surviving Caddoans would somewhat modify the impressions gained from these early writers.

These grass lodges above described were the permanent dwellings. When on the chase, temporary tents of skins were used. An eighteenth-century witness [Fray Miguel de Santa Maria] tells of this class of tent used by the Yatasís, a related tribe, outside their regular villages. "A little before reaching this pueblo, I came upon an Indian chief, in a field tent [*chocita de campo*], which they make of the skins or hides of deer they kill. It was so small that there was hardly room in it for the bench [*tapestle*] of reeds covered with a buffalo (skin) that constituted his bed. There was another tent [*campito*] containing the light, which these people never lack."[15]

House Interiors

Inside, the permanent houses were arranged to accommodate several families and [a fire] made of large logs placed end to end. In cold weather it was kept constantly burning, and other fires were built under the beds to keep the sleepers warm. Smoke apparently was no inconvenience.[16] Each family

[14] French, ed. *Historical Collections*, 1: 149.

[15] Fray Miguel de Santa Maria to Viceroy Antonio de Bucareli, July 21, 1774, in "Expediente sobre la dolosa y fingida paz de las Naciones del Norte," AGN, Historia, vol. 93, fol. 160.

[16] French, ed., *Historical Collections*, 1: 148; Espinosa, *Chrónica*, p. 440. "Which ordinarily never dies out in these cabins (*cabanes*) because the savages put on it large trees, which keep burning a long time. When they are cut the savages draw the two ends together, with wood placed around (*avec du mesme bois autour*). I have seen them place trees requiring eight or nine men to carry, so that, although there was little wood, it made a good fire." Margry, ed. and trans., *Découvertes*, 3: 351; French, ed., *Historical Collections*, 4: 204; Espinosa, *Chrónica*, p. 440; French, ed. *Historical Collections*, 1: 148.

had its nook or corner, with bed, food supply, and utensils to itself, although the family spaces do not seem to have been separated by solid partitions. The raised beds of the Hasinais were something early observers never saw farther west.[17] Those in the house of the Nabedache caddi were thus described by Massanet (1690): "Ranged around one half of the house, inside, there are ten beds, which consist of a rug made of reeds, laid on (a platform supported by) four forked sticks. Over the rug they spread buffalo skins, on which they sleep. At the head and foot of the bed is attached another carpet, forming a sort of arch, which, lined with a very brilliantly colored piece of reed matting, makes what bears some resemblance to a very pretty alcove."[18] These beds were about a yard high and were separated by reed mats, each forming a sort of bower.[19] Sometimes, apparently, they were covered with long unwoven reeds instead of with mats and skins.[20]

That part of the houses not occupied by beds was devoted to domestic utensils and the storage of food. The principal feature in this connection was the platform or platforms (or compartments, as Espinosa calls them), six or seven feet high and made of stakes, poles, and reeds. Continuing the description of the Nabedache caddi's house, Massanet said, after describing the beds: "In the other half of the house, where there are no beds, there are some shelves about two *varas* high and on them are ranged large round baskets made of reeds, in which

[17] Thus the four characteristics of the Hasinais that struck Espinosa's attention, when in 1716 he first saw them after traveling six hundred miles from the Rio Grande, were that "they were settled permanently on their land, built their houses with great care and with high beds for all, and with compartments of wood where they have their baskets of nuts, maize, and beans for the whole year." Espinosa, Diario, 1716, AGN *Historia*, vol. 394, fol. 131.

[18] Massanet, "Carta," p. 303.

[19] Margry, ed. and trans., *Découvertes*, 3: 345; French, ed., *Historical Collections*, 4: 204, says, "The beds are ranged around the cabin, three or four feet from the ground."

[20] Margry, ed. and trans., *Découvertes*, 3: 345.

they keep their corn, nuts, acorns, beans, etc.; a row of very large earthen pots like our earthen jars, these pots being used only to make the *atole* when there is a large crowd on the occasion of some ceremony; and six wooden mortars for pounding the corn in rainy weather, for, when it is fair, they grind it in the courtyard."[21] Joutel mentioned a similar though slightly different arrangement among the Nasonis. "There is a large platform above the door made of pieces of wood set *de bout* with others across and with reeds laid and pressed close together. On this they place their corn in the ear. There is another platform opposite upon which they place the casks or tuns, made of reeds and bark, in which they put their shelled corn, beans, nuts, acorns, and other things. Under the platform they put their pottery. Each family has its private casks. On the right and left they have their beds."[22]

Tables were not used for eating, but the houses were well supplied with low stools, each made of a single solid piece of wood. Inside the houses of the Chenesi and the caddis there were special raised platforms or tables, with foot benches at the side, on which the priests performed religious ceremonies, and, as was stated above, in the houses of the caddis and principal men there were beds and stools specially reserved for the Chenesi.

The only evidence that I have seen of an attempt at architectural decorations is the capping of the houses with the fanciful grass peaks, which probably had a religious meaning, and the statement that over the door inside of the Nabedache caddi's house there was a "little mound of pebbles very prettily arranged."[23] What was the purpose of the latter I cannot say, but it also may have had some religious significance.

We must remember that the house and interior arrange-

[21] Massanet, "Carta," pp. 303–304.

[22] Margry, ed. and trans., *Découvertes,* 3: 393–94; French, ed., *Historical Collections,* 1: 149.

[23] Fray Francisco de Jesús María Casañas, Relación, August 15, 1691, AGN, *Historia,* vol. 394, fols. 4–5.

ments here described by Joutel, Massanet, and Espinosa are those of the leading members of Hasinai society, and that several witnesses tell us that the houses of these head men were larger, better built, and more elaborately furnished than those of less prominent households.[24]

Public Buildings—Assembly Houses

The most conspicuous of the buildings other than the dwellings were the general assembly houses that were erected in some if not all of the principal villages. In them were held public rejoicings, preparations for war, and receptions of distinguished guests. They are mentioned in the three of the Hasinai villages concerning which we have fullest details: the Nabedaches, the Neches, and the Nasonis, and it may be inferred that other villages possessed them.

In describing his reception at the Nabedache village, Joutel says that he was conducted first to the house of the chief, then to a "large cabin, which they had about a quarter of a league from there, where they held their rejoicings and made preparations for the war." There he and his companions were made to sit on mats, beside the "*anciens*" and were given food and a smoke.[25] Next day in the Neche village five leagues away they were received in the same manner, first in the house of the chief, then in the "*cabane d'assemble.*" "They call it thus because they make these cabins when they prepare for war and hold in them festivities to incite the young men to go."[26] This last passage might indicate a temporary character for the assembly houses, particularly since at the time when Joutel was among them they were preparing for war with the Canohatinnos. This general assembly house seems in some cases to have been distinct from the house in which the chief held his council meetings. The assembly house mentioned by Joutel as

[24] Espinosa, *Chrónica*, p. 423; Massanet, "Carta," p. 303.
[25] Margry, ed. and trans., *Découvertes*, 3: 343.
[26] Ibid., 344–45.

in the Nabedache village was a quarter of a league from the caddi's house, but the council house was close by. The council building was a large one, and the architecture apparently was different from that of the round grass lodge. Telling of his experience at the house of the Nabedache caddi, Massanet says: "Soon I noticed, outside the yard, opposite the door of the governor's house, another building, a long one in which no inmates could be seen. I asked who dwelt in it and what purpose it served and was told that the captains (chief men) were lodged in that house when the governor called them to a meeting."[27] There is some indication that sometimes these meetings held by the caddi were at his dwelling, for Casañas says that the canaha calls the elders to the house of the caddi when they go to hunt or to war.[28] However, this "house of the caddi" may mean his council house.

Near the council house at the Nabedache village there was a smaller dwelling. Massanet was informed that it was for the servants of the "captains" when they were assembled, "for there is a law providing that when the governor assembles the captains each one shall bring his page and they follow this custom."[29] Massanet evidently failed to understand what he saw in this particular.

Corn Dryers

Joutel described a class of structure at the Nasoni village that was specialized for agricultural purposes, and which no one mentions at other Hasinai villages, though it may have existed elsewhere. It was [a] primitive corncrib. "These people," he said, "have also before their cabins a large platform, which is raised ten or twelve feet. On it they put their ears of corn to dry after they are cut, and they are careful to sweep it every day."[30]

[27] Massanet, "Carta," p. 304.
[28] Casañas, Relación, fol. 7.
[29] Massanet, "Carta," p. 304.
[30] Margry, ed. and trans., *Découvertes*, 3: 394.

Temples

To the Christian priests who in early days labored among the Hasinais, the native cult and its instruments were especially noteworthy matters; consequently they made frequent mention of the Hasinai "mosques" (*mesquitas*), designating them by a term reflecting the long Spanish struggle against the Mohammedan. In some cases, perhaps, what one witness called a temple was identical with a building that another called an assembly house or council house, but in others they are clearly distinct. The buildings called temples seem to have exhibited no marked peculiarities of architecture, being similar in material and structure to the dwellings and differing mainly in the furnishings. Thus Espinosa described the chenesi's temple or "fire house" as large, round, and thatched with grass.[31] Besides this main temple there were the house of the coninisi and tribal or subgroup temples at different places in the confederacy. [Their uses and furnishings will be presented under the heading "Religious Beliefs and Customs."]

Arts and Crafts

In the arts and crafts the Hasinais had not reached a high stage of development compared with the most advanced native Americans, such as some of the peoples of central Mexico, for example, yet they were far removed from the most primitive Indians and had numerous manufactured implements, utensils, and fabrics.

The leading arts were making pottery, bows and arrows, baskets, mats, dressing skins, and securing salt. Much of this handiwork was done in inclement weather and in the winter months by both men and women while they were sitting around the fire, but there was, nevertheless, a clear distinction between women's tasks and men's tasks.[32]

[31] Espinosa, *Chrónica*, pp. 424–25.
[32] Casañas, Relación, fol. 13.

Pottery

The pottery was made, as usual, by the women. Espinosa in enumerating the tasks of the Hasinai women, says, "and with their hands they make of clay all that they need for their manual work."[33] They were skillful in making clay cooking vessels, receptacles for storing flour, grain, nuts and fruits, plates for eating, pitchers and jugs for holding liquids, and other utensils for domestic use.[34] By Casañas, who was acquainted with Mexican pottery, their work was pronounced good.[35] From the Hasinai mounds excellent specimens of this ware have been taken in recent years. It is well shaped, prettily decorated with symbolic figures, and successfully colored.

Baskets and Mats

Basketry, it seems, was more highly developed than pottery making, and it displayed considerably advancement in the decorative art. The larger baskets or tuns used for storing the food supply were made of canes, reeds, and bark.[36] Also made of reeds (*otates*) were handsome *panniers* for saddle bags, and sieves and platters for sifting flour.[37] Highly decorated baskets and chests were used in the temples for religious purposes, which will be discussed in that connection. The best mats made by the women were closely woven and sometimes were brilliantly colored. They were used for rugs in the homes, in the temples, and in the council houses as well as for beds, clothing, and curtains.[38]

[33] Espinosa, *Chrónica*, p. 436.

[34] Casañas, Relación, fols. 2, 5; Margry, ed. and trans., *Découvertes*, 3: 353; Massanet, "Carta," p. 304.

[35] Casañas, Relación, fol. 2.

[36] Massanet, "Carta," p. 303; Espinosa, *Chrónica*,, p. 422. Among the Nasonis, Joutel noted the use of bark in making these casks and for eating platters. He did not mention these bark platters among the other Hasinais, but they were probably used. Margry, ed. and trans., *Découvertes*, 3: 393.

[37] Margry, ed. and trans., *Découvertes*, 3: 367.

[38] Ibid., p. 345; Massanet, "Carta," p. 303.

Skin Dressing

As everywhere among Indians who hunted large game, skins were skillfully and beautifully tanned and colored. Both men and women knew how to prepare them, and both sexes regularly took part in the work.[39] Skins were fashioned into all kinds of clothing and were used for curtains, mats, beddings, and numerous other purposes.[40] Clothing made of them was very soft. According to Espinosa, a process of dyeing buckskins a beautifully shiny black, making them look like very fine cloth, was known only to the Hasinais. The garments made of skins were often highly decorated with colors and ornaments.[41]

Agricultural Implements

Among manufactured agricultural implements were hoes or picks made by inserting a bone or a sharp stick in a split handle and tying it with bark or other fiber. From Espinosa we infer that the usual native hoe or pick was of walnut (nogal) hardened in the fire.[42] The favorite bone of the prairie Indians for this purpose, and perhaps that of the Hasinais also, was the shoulder blade of the buffalo.[43] In speaking of their funeral customs, Casañas mentions the digging of graves with adzes, without indicating what they are made of.[44] From our knowledge of other Indians or similar culture and habits, and from the archaeological finds in their country, we may suppose that stone spades and hoes were used by the Hasinais, although no mention is made of them in the early records.[45]

[39] Casañas, Relación, fol. 6.
[40] Ibid.; Margry, ed. and trans., Découvertes, 3: 341.
[41] Espinosa, Chrónica,, pp. 432, 435: "Q. solo alli las saben tenir."
[42] Ibid., p. 421: "Azadones de madera de nogal tostado."
[43] Margry, ed. and trans., Découvertes, 3: 364.
[44] Casañas, Relación, fol. 20.
[45] Hodge, ed., Handbook 1: 26–27.

Mortars and Sieves

For grinding corn, sunflower seeds, tuqui, and other things into flour, they used wooden mortars. Joutel thus describes the process of making mortars and of grinding: "The women parch it and then grind it into very fine flour. If the savages had mills it would lighten their work greatly, since this is a laborious task. They have large mortars that they make from the trunk of a tree, hollowed out with fire to a certain depth, after which they scrape and shape it. As many as four women grind the corn. Each one has a large pestle nearly five feet long, and they keep time like blacksmiths when they strike upon an anvil. When they have ground a certain time, they take out the flour and other women pass it through little sieves, which they make very well of large reeds. And when they wish to have it very fine, they have small flat baskets [vannettes] upon which they shake the flour, where the finest remains attached to the bottom, the coarser flour (gruau) and the bran coming to the top. In this way they make it as fine as possible, and as fine as I have ever seen in France or elsewhere."[46] In pleasant weather the flour was ground outside, but in bad weather this was done indoors. In the house of the Nabedache caddi, Massanet saw six wooden mortars.[47]

Weapons

Apparently the native weapons of the Hasinais were mainly bows and arrows, war clubs, shields, and perhaps some kind of a lance or spear. Espinosa writes, "In these wars . . . they formerly used bows and arrows and their shields." The latter, which were of buffalo hide, they carried on the left arm. Joutel tells us that when he was met by the Indians near the Nabedache village "some had bows with several arrows, and others

[46] Margry, ed. and trans., Découvertes, 3: 367.
[47] Massanet, "Carta," p. 304. Mortars "muy curiosos" are mentioned by Espinosa, Chrónica, pp. 435–36.

had war clubs [*un casse teste*]." Besides these, eight of the leading men were armed with "sword blades" (*lames d'espesses*), which had great bunches of feathers at the points. These blades were "square like those of Spain."[48] These of course were of European make. Casañas tells us about the use of an "*espada sin guarnicion*"[49] by a Hasinai priest at a funeral ceremonial. Just what it was it is difficult to say. Within a short time after the coming of the Spaniards and the French, these native weapons were largely displaced by French guns. As early as about 1718 Espinosa counted over ninety guns in the possession of the Indians at one mission.[50]

Cutting Tools

The implements most lacked by these Indians were cutting tools. Casañas said that their hardest tasks were clearing land and building houses, because of this lack,[51] and he prophesied that the Spaniards would find a ready trade in such things. Though horses were scarce among them, at this time they willingly exchanged one for a hatchet or two.[52] Before the coming of the French, the Hasinais seem to have gotten very few of such things from the Spanish. Upon this point Joutel, speaking of the Ebahamos near the Colorado, says, "It does not appear that they have much trade with the latter [the Spaniards] since they have neither an ax nor a knife." In speaking of the agricultural implements of the Hasinais, he positively says they have no tools of iron.[53] "That which I learned very

[48] Margry, ed. and trans., *Découvertes*, 3, 341–42. Penicaut tells of the warrior's equipment in 1714, after horses had been secured in plenty. Ibid., 5: 502.

[49] Casañas, Relación, fol. 21.

[50] Espinosa, *Chrónica,*, p. 435–36.

[51] Casañas, Relación, fol. 11.

[52] French, ed., *Historical Collections*, 4: 204.

[53] Margry., ed. and trans., *Découvertes*, 3: 292, 364.

well was their liking for the knives and axes, which they love greatly, and of which they have great need, not having any of them, although they have been to the Spaniards, which shows that the latter do not give them much.[54]

For the lighter kinds of work, such as shaving the beard, shells were used for cutting. As the country of the Hasinais did not furnish shells, they had to procure them from the coast, through the littoral coast tribes. Cabeza de Vaca (1528–36) mentions going inland from the Gulf shore as much as forty or fifty leagues, carrying seashells, cockles, shells used to cut fruit, shell beads, and so on. In exchange he brought back hides and red ochre, flint, glue, hard canes, and deer's hair.[55] The fact that he brought back deer skins and red ochre might point to a trade with the Hasinais, because their country was noted for both these products. Moreover, the red ochre country did not extend very far south of the Hasinai country and was relatively limited. But as Cabeza de Vaca does not mention any Indian dwellings that would correspond with the large grass lodges of the Hasinais, I think it improbable that he penetrated so far inland himself. He perhaps traded with intermediaries between the coast Indians and the Hasinais, possibly the Orcoquisacas and Bidais.

In the early seventeenth century many coast Indians, allies of the Hasinais, came each year after the Hasinai harvest, to trade and feast, bringing shells and no doubt other coast products.[56]

[54] Ibid., 3: 349.

[55] Fanny Bandelier, trans. *The Journey of Álvar Nuñez Cabeza de Vaca and His Companions from Florida to the Pacific, 1528–1536*, p. 75.

[56] Espinosa, *Chrónica*, p. 437. "The same policy (*politica*) they show towards the tribes who live to the south very near the shore of the Gulf of Mexico, who are accustomed to come as allies of the Texas in time of war. To keep them friendly they entertain them every year after harvest, which is the time when many families of men and women come to visit the Assinais. It is also the time when they trade with each other for those things they lack in their pueblos."

Musical Instruments

Various sorts of musical instruments were in use among the Hasinais. Espinosa found in the "Fire House" many bones of cranes, which served as flutes or fifes, and others of carved reeds.[57] The medicine men used fifes of curved *palellos* and *sizuras* like a "cascabel de vibora y este palellos puesto en hueco sobre un cuero, hace consonacia de nada menos, que infierno."[58] Another instrument was a rattle made of the "*guaje*" or calabash with small stones inside.[59] A drum was made of a hollow log and beaten by eight men. Espinosa described it as follows: "Teniendo un madero entenado, y en hueco, y cubierta de verdes ramos por cima, elijen ocho Indios robusto, que sentados a propocion con unos moderos, a dos manos, forman a tambor del madero hueco, al compaz de la calabaza que tocan los viejos, los cantores, y cantatrices."[60]

Wood Carving

Among the handicrafts that had assumed the form of an art was wood carving. The extent to which it was practiced does not appear, but some elaborate specimens of this art are recorded by the early witnesses. Espinosa describes, for example, among the furniture of the fire temple, carved reed musical instruments and "four or five plates or vessels like round porringers, made of black wood, very carefully carved. Their four feet are carved, some in the form of little ducks with both head and tail [represented]; and some with the tail and feet of a crocodile or lizard."[61]

[57] Ibid., p. 425.
[58] Ibid., p. 427.
[59] Ibid.
[60] Ibid., p. 433.
[61] Ibid., p. 425.

Miscellaneous Handicrafts

Handicrafts extended to the making of various musical instruments. Other classes of artifacts mentioned in the early records are canoes, rafts, ropes of bark used to tether dogs, fasten the poles of the houses, or tie up candles,[62] strings of rabbits hair used by men and women in the coiffure,[63] and biers and coffins used to carry and bury their dead. Casañas said that they carried their dead on an open bier (*carrera abierta*),[64] but what it was made of he does not say. Neither does it appear whether or not the coffins were of skins or of wood. For dyeing, for painting the body, and for other purposes, various products were utilized either in their natural state or after preparation. Among the products thus used were red ochre,[65] white clay, coal, and a certain red plant that abounded in the whole country,[66] but which I have not identified.

[62] Margry, ed. and trans., *Découvertes* 3: 353, 364.

[63] Espinosa, *Chrónica*, p. 435.

[64] Casañas, Relación, fols. 20–21.

[65] Casañas tells us that the Hasinais were famous for their red ochre supply, and that other tribes came there from long distances to procure it. *Ibid.*, fol. 2.

[66] Espinosa, *Chrónica*, pp. 434–35.

6

Dress and Adornment

Ordinary Dress

The testimony of early witnesses makes it certain that custom required Hasinai women to wear at least a minimum amount of bodily covering, but that the social code was less exacting with the men on this score, although it seems that to go entirely without clothing was not common even with them. To quote from Joutel a passage awkwardly translated by [Benjamin] French, "The country of those Indians being generally subject to no cold, almost all of them (the men) go naked, unless when the north wind blows, then they cover themselves with a bullock's hide, or goat's (deer's) skin cured. The women wear nothing but a skin, mat, or clout, hanging round them like a petticoat, and reaching down half way their legs, which hides their nakedness before or behind." The same authority tells us that on ordinary occasions they wore no head covering.[1]

Casañas's statement, which has greater value, emphasizes more the necessity of clothing for the women and less the practice of nudism by the men. "The ordinary dress of these poor people," he says, "consists of deer skins and buffalo hides, which are very well tanned. In very hot weather the men go naked in their houses,[2] but the women even when very small,

[1] Benjamin F. French, ed., *Historical Collections of Louisiana*, 1: 150.
[2] Or "In very hot weather and in their houses the men go naked." The Spanish is "En tiempo de muchos calores, en sus casas los hombres hordina-

always go covered from the waist down."[3] Again, speaking of both men and women, he remarked "the most they customarily have is a poor deer or buffalo skin."[4] Espinosa's statement bearing on the same subject implies that even the men always wore a slight covering. "In hot weather," he says, "the men go about with only a flap or furbelow (*cendal*), which covers them in front, and nothing else, and in cold weather they are protected by buffalo skins very well dressed and painted. . . . On the other hand, all the women clothe themselves all the year round with very great modesty, since with garments made of two dressed deerskins they cover themselves entirely from the feet to the throat."[5] It will be noted that, while there is comparatively close agreement between Joutel and Casañas on the scanty garments of the women, Espinosa assigns them clothing, regularly worn and covering the upper as well as the lower portion of the body.

Specific instances of meeting men unburdened with garments support the generalization above given as to their habits. Massanet was first greeted by the Nabedache caddi in a state of nature and fresh from a bath in a creek, but "that night it was arranged to provide the governor with garments, in order that he might enter his village clothed, so that his people might see how highly we thought of him."[6] On a different occasion Joutel was met at the same village by three Indians, two of them nude, and the third incongruously arrayed

---

riamente andan desnudos," which would easily admit of the mistake of leaving out *y* after *calores*. Fray Francisco de Jesús María Casañas, Relación, August 15, 1691, AGN, Historia, vol. 394, fol. 5.

[3] Ibid.

[4] Ibid., fol. 6.

[5] Isidro Felix de Espinosa, *Chrónica apostólica, y seráphica de todos los colegios de propaganda fide de esta Nueva-España*, p. 435.

[6] Damián Massanet, "Carta de Don Damian Mazanet a Don Carlos de Siguenza y Góngora sobre el Descubrimiento de la Bahia de Espiritu Santo," trans. Lilia M. Casis, *Quarterly* of the Texas State Historical Association 2 (April, 1899): 302.

in various elements of Spanish garb.[7] It took only a year's residence among the Hasinais to accustom the French deserters from La Salle's party to a state of almost entire nakedness,[8] a habit which they must have borrowed from their hosts. At certain religious ceremonials the men taking part were required to remove their clothing.[9]

Everywhere the Indian was pretty closely limited in the matter of clothing, as in habitations and food supply, by his immediate surroundings. Accordingly the materials most usually employed by the Hasinais for clothing and bedding were tanned deerskins,[10] which were very plentiful in their immediate vicinity, tanned buffalo skins, and reed or grass matting. Among the Nasonis garments of feathers were used, apparently for protection as well as for ornament, and it is not unlikely that they were similarly used by other Hasinais. Speaking of Ruter, a deserter from the La Salle party who had lived a year among the Nasonis, Joutel says: "It seemed as if he had been a savage for ten years. His whole dress consisted of a miserable garment which the savages of the district where they had been fashioned from turkey feathers and adjusted with little strings, which they make very well."[11] From another passage, we learn that these feather garments were worn over the shoulder, probably like a blanket.[12] Before the visit of La Salle to this country the Hasinai women had obtained from the Spaniards a small quantity of coarse blue cloth, of which color they were extremely fond and were using it to make skirts,[13] as well as for decorative and other purposes.

As to the different kinds of garments made out of these fabrics, information goes little beyond what is given above. There were the men's clouts, the women's skirts, the blankets,

[7]Pierre Margry, ed. and trans., *Découvertes et éstablissements des français dans l'ouest et dans le sud de l'Amérique Septentrionale, 1614–1754*, 3: 339.
[8]Ibid., 3: 350, 356.
[9]Casañas, Relación, fols. 17, 21.
[10]Massanet, "Carta," p. 311.
[11]Margry, ed. and trans., *Découvertes*, 3: 353.
[12]Ibid., 3: 366.
[13]Ibid., p. 349.

and the moccasins worn by men and women alike. An outside shirt worn by the women and perhaps by the men, seems to have been made and adjusted somewhat like the Mexican's serape.

That these garments were often carefully and even tastefully made and decorated, we gather from passages like the following: "These deerskins are very black and shiny, and only here is it known how to dye them.[14] They look like fine cloth. To give them a more pleasing appearance they border all the edges with very small beads (cuentecillas), which are grown in a state of nature on certain plants. Making holes in them, . . . they sew them easily on their deerskins. With another large deerskin, well dyed and open in the middle for the head, they cover the breast and shoulders and the body to the waist. They cut all the edges like a fringe, which makes the garment very comely."[15]

Coiffure

Hair dressing was a matter of importance with most Indians, and different tribes were readily known from each other by this feature.[16] Thus the Apaches, who wore their hair long, were easily distinguished from the tribes the Spaniards called the Norteños, including the Hasinais and Wichitas, who characteristically cut most of their hair except a scalp lock.[17] Our witnesses do not give us much light on the totemic or ceremonial significance of hair dressing among these people, but they agree essentially in their statements as to the prevailing customs, varying, however, in details. Joutel said that the larger part of the Hasinais cut off their hair except a lock, like the Turks, which they fastened to or twisted around a stick

[14] See above concerning preparation of animal skins.
[15] Espinosa, Chrónica, p. 435.
[16] Frederick Webb Hodge, ed., The Handbook of American Indians North of Mexico, Bureau of American Ethnology Bulletin no. 30 (1907), 1: 524–26.
[17] Felipe de Neve to Domingo Cabello, February 7, 1784, Bexar Archives, reel 15, frame 0632–34.

and hung on one side.[18] Casañas tells us that they were very fond of fine and well-groomed hair, but that those not so favored carefully shaved the head, leaving in the center a long lock reaching to the waist. Espinosa's statement is apparently self-contradictory as to the closeness with which the hair, other than the scalp lock, was shaved, for he says, "They do not wear the hair long, for all cut it at the root (*a cercen*), leaving it about two fingers long, and keeping it very even and smooth. In the middle of the head, they let grow a thin braid like the Chinese, and in it they carefully put the most beautiful feathers, whereupon each one thinks he is like *un pimpollo.*" Great care was also taken, we are told, to remove the beard and eyebrows with a conch shell.[19] Delisle tells us that the Kadohadacho men cut their hair like Capuchins, greased it with bear's fat and, when they attended a ceremonial, put on it down of swan or bustard, painted red,[20] thus making a very fine show.

Though, contrary to the customs of most civilized peoples, coiffure was less important to the Hasinai women than to the men, even by them it was by no means neglected. They wore their hair very carefully combed, formed into a braid, folded or doubled up, and carefully tied at the head with a slender string made of rabbit's hair, dyed bright red with a plant found everywhere in that country.[21]

Delisle asserts that the Kadohadacho women very carefully parted their hair in front.[22]

Holiday and Ceremonial Dress

If, under ordinary circumstances, these Indians wore little clothing unless more was required for protection from the

[18] Margry, ed. and trans., *Découvertes*, 3: 356.
[19] Ibid.; Espinosa, *Chrónica*, p. 435.
[20] Margry, ed. and trans., *Découvertes*, 3: 413; French, ed., *Historical Collections*, 1: 169.
[21] Espinosa, *Chrónica*, p. 435; French, ed., *Historical Collections*, 1: 150.
[22] Margry, ed. and trans., *Découvertes*, 3: 413.

cold, on ceremonial and holiday occasions they presented a great variety of personal adornments. Then, the tanned skins, at other times moderately decorated or not at all, were dyed in different bright colors and adorned with various ornaments. On these occasions the people rigged themselves out in garbs having symbolical significance, or according to personal whims, some appearing as gay, others as horrible as possible.[23] One's special garments we are told were carefully preserved for these particular uses. Speaking of one of these Hasinai ceremonials, Espinosa says: "When the day for it arrives, they bring out all their best baize garments, which they preserve for this purpose, very soft deerskins, with fringes ornamented with white beads, and other very black deerskins, carefully besprinkled with those beads, bracelets, and necklaces, which are used only on this and other ceremonial days."[24]

When the Spaniards arrived in East Texas they found that among the Hasinais blue was a favorite color in their choice of fabrics, a fact that was noted by several observers, and which was explained in various ways. Massanet attributed it to an ecstatic visitation to the Hasinais made by the Venerable Mother María de Agreda, who dressed in blue,[25] but Casañas

[23] Casañas, Relación, fol. 5.

[24] Espinosa, Chrónica, p. 432.

[25] Casañas, Relación, fol. 10. This love for blue cloth was attested by Domingo Ramon, "Derrotero," AGN, Historia, vol. 27, fol. 156. The story of the tradition that this sister had in ecstasy visited and converted the Xumanes (Jumanos) of New Mexico before 1639 is told by Edmond J. P. Schmidt, "Ven, María Jesús de Agreda: A Correction," Quarterly of the Texas State Historical Association 1 (October, 1897): 121–24. Its application by Massanet to the Hasinais' fondness for blue cloth is seen in the following extract from his story of his visit to the Hasinais in 1690: "While we were at the Tejas village, after we had distributed clothing to the Indians and to the governor of the Tejas, that governor asked me one evening for a piece of blue baize to make a shroud in which to bury his mother when she died. I told him that cloth would be more suitable, and he answered that he did not want any other color than blue. I then asked him what mysterious reason he had for preferring the blue color, and in reply he said that they were fond of that color, particularly for burial clothes, because in times past they had been visited by a very beautiful woman who used to come down

said it was due solely to the fact that blue was the color of the sky. The difference between the two will probably never be settled.

Head Dress

With the men the head dress was a matter of prime importance on ceremonial occasions. The favorite articles used for this purpose were feathers gaily painted, but even deer's horns were used.[26] In describing his reception at the Nabedache village, Joutel said that the committee came out to meet him with bunches of variously painted feathers worn upon their heads like turbans.[27] Feathers were sometimes carried in the hand as well as worn upon the head and were preserved for ceremonial occasions in hollow reeds.

Ornaments

Ornaments were prized alike by men and by women. In the selection of ornaments the Hasinais showed a childish preference for what would jingle and make a noise. Casañas noted that their ear pendants resembled those worn by the Mexicans in the heathen state.[28] They wore round the neck or attached

from the hills, dressed in blue garments, and that they wished to do as that woman had done. On my asking whether that had been long since, the governor said that it had been before his time, but that his mother, who was aged, had seen that woman, as had also the other older people. From this it is easily to be seen that they referred to the Madre María de Jesús de Agreda, who was very frequently in those regions, as she herself acknowledged to the Father Custodian of New Mexico, her last visit having been made in 1631, this last fact being evident from her own statement, made to the Father Custodian of New Mexico." Massanet, "Carta," p. 312.

[26] Espinosa, Chrónica, p. 435.

[27] Margry, ed. and trans., Découvertes, 3: 342.

[28] We are told that the Kadohadacho women wore "little locks of fine red hair, which they made fast to their ears, in the nature of pendants." French, ed., Historical Collections, 1: 169.

to their skin, blankets, white shells like glass beads, which they found in the field, snake rattles, and deer hoofs. Before the coming of the Spanish missionaries they had obtained indirectly from the Spaniards or other nations such things as hawks-bells, shells, etc.[29] These they suspended with their native gew-gaws round the neck or sewed them to their buckskin garments in such a way as to make the most noise.[30] This love for ornament was the key to much of the hold acquired by the Spaniards and French over the Hasinai natives.

Tattooing and Painting

Among features of personal adornment even more noticeable than head dress and ornaments, were the painting and tattooing of face and body, a custom apparently common to all the Texas Caddoans, with certain characteristics distinguishing the northern from the southern division. Tattooing was not, of course, connected alone with ceremonial, because when once tattooed the marks were permanent. But it usually, no doubt, had some symbolical significance. Tattooing was performed by the very painful process of pricking the skin and forcing under it very fine charcoal.[31] It was practiced by both men and women, but apparently more often by the women. They marked their arms and bodies from waist to shoulders with various designs. A favorite custom was to adorn their breasts with geometrical figures and their shoulders with flowers.[32] It would seem from a passage in French's edition of Joutel's *Journal* that they even tattooed their faces, for it is therein said that "These [Kadohadacho] women have their

[29] Casañas, Relación, fol. 5. Joutel was met at the Nabedache village by a party of Indians wearing hawks' bells. Margry, ed. and trans., *Découvertes*, 3: 342. They might have been supplied by La Salle.

[30] Casañas, Relación, fol. 11.

[31] Margry, ed. and trans., *Découvertes*, 3: 349.

[32] These Joutel called "du point d'Espagne"; ibid; Casañas, Relación, fol. 11; Espinosa, *Chrónica*, p. 435.

faces still more disfigured than the others we have seen before, for they made several streaks or scars in them, whereas the others [the Hasinais] had but one."[33] Espinosa bears this out by saying that the Hasinai women "have no more than one stripe in the middle of the face, but they decorate with great care their breasts and their arms. This work is done with the thorn when they are tender girls."[34] The men were fond of tattooing themselves with figures of birds and animals, and sometimes they pricked half the body with irregular zig-zag figures.[35]

Painting face and body was usually a more temporary thing and the accompaniment of some special event, like the reception of a stranger, a social or religious ceremonial, or going to war. The custom of painting is usually explained by the love of decoration or by symbolism, but Casañas, speaking of the Hasinais, gave an additional explanation, saying: "Their way of painting themselves in some of their mitotes is ridiculous, and to go to war they all gather in one place painted in different colors. They say they do this in order not to be known by their enemies. They do the same when they have a guest from another tribe and for the same reason."[36]

The materials used for face decorations were various. Joutel was met near the Nabedache village by Indians with visages daubed, some with black and some with red for the Hasinais were in the midst of a red ochre bed so famous that Indians of distant tribes were in the habit of coming to procure the com-

[33] French, ed., *Historical Collections*, 1: 169. The statement in Margry by Delisle is different. He says, "They mar the breast and face by making marks on them as I have already said (of the Hasinais and the Nasonis); Margry, ed. and trans., *Découvertes*, 3: 413.

[34] Espinosa, *Chrónica*, p. 435.

[35] Margry, *Découvertes*, 3: 349. Ruter, a deserter from La Salle who had been among the Nasonis came to visit Joutel both tattooed and painted. Joutel remarks, "But that which I most of all wondered at was that he was tattooed [*fait piquer*] like them and marked on the face, so that he was almost nothing different from them except that he was not so alert"; ibid., 3: 353.

[36] Casañas, *Relación*, fol. 5.

modity.[37] For black paint coals were used.[38] White earth was utilized for giving the face a ghastly hue.[39] After contact with the whites, vermillion was a favorite coloring substance and was never omitted from the trader's pack. Espinosa tells of its being mixed with bear's fat for face painting, the fat being used, no doubt, to cause the vermillion to stick.

[37] Margry, ed. and trans., *Découvertes,* 3: 342.
[38] Casañas, Relación, fol. 2.
[39] Espinosa, *Chrónica,* pp. 433–34. See also p. 99 for use of white earth in deer hunts.

7

Religious Beliefs and Customs

No white man ever understood the psychology of an Indian, and the most difficult task in studying their institutions is to correctly interpret their social and religious customs, for one may see the externals of a ceremonial without understanding its meaning. This difficulty, in full measure, is encountered in studying the Hasinais. The early witnesses saw much of their ceremonial and heard many of their traditions, but we cannot be sure that they explained them correctly; and the few remaining survivors of these Indians have lost so much of their primitive culture that it is hard to identify modern with older traditions and customs.

With these difficulties in view, together with that of my own limited knowledge of Indian ceremonial, I have restricted the pages that follow mainly to an effort to record faithfully, without attempt at interpretation, what early witnesses reported concerning Hasinai religious beliefs and ceremonial, in the hope that the accounts here set forth, may be of use, as raw material, to the specialist in this field of anthropology. Of course, we must not forget that the witnesses in all probability read into what they saw many of their own notions of the universe.

Ideas of God

In studying the religious beliefs of the Hasinais we naturally first ask, "What were their ideas concerning deity?" The combined testimony of our best early witnesses conveys the impression that although they personified a multitude of things, clothing them with mysterious powers over the various affairs of mankind, yet they believed in a great being, resident in the sky, whom they regarded as infinitely more powerful than other spirits or deities.

Caddi Ayo

Casañas went so far as to say that they believed in "only one God," but other direct testimony of his own, like that of others, shows a belief in many supernatural powers.[1] The principal deity, belief in whom was common to all the Hasinais,[2] we are told, they regarded in the light of a great chief, which the name they gave him seems to have meant. According to Espinosa he was called Caddi, or Ayo, or Caddi Ayo, "Which is the same as the Chief Above," or "great chief" [*capitán grande*]. It is of interest to note in this connection that "Cachao Ayo" was their expression for "the sky."[3] Massanet tells us that they called him "Ayimat Caddi—which signified in the language, Great Captain." Continuing, he says, "This was the name he [a Hasinai priest] gave to God, for, since the only rank or title they know is that of captain, they call 'Great Captain' him whom they consider great above all things."[4] According to Casañas he was "Caddi Aymay," which was a title akin to "*ay mayxoya,*" or "great man," the name formally conferred upon one who had won honors in wars. Following

[1] Fray Francisco de Jesús María Casañas, Relación, August 15, 1691, AGN, Historia, vol. 394, fols. 14–16.

[2] Espinosa says it extended to "toda esta Numerosa Nacion de los Assinais, q tienen con el mismo idioma mas de catorce, o quince Parcialidades." Isidro Felix de Espinosa, Chrónica apostólica, y seráphica de todos los colegios de propaganda fide de esta Nueva-España, p. 423.

[3] Ibid., pp. 423–25.

[4] Damián Massanet, "Carta de Don Damian Mazanet a Don Carlos de Siguenza y Góngora sobre el Descubrimiento de la Bahia de Espiritu Santo," trans. Lilia M. Casis, Quarterly of the Texas State Historical Association 2 (April, 1899): 306–307.

Espinosa, as the best qualified witness, his distinctive name, therefore, was Ayo.

Attributes of Caddi Ayo

Caddi Ayo was creator of all things, though himself born of woman.[6] He could punish and reward, but was a being to be propitiated and kept well disposed rather than to be venerated and loved.[7] He could give or withhold good health, plentiful harvests, or success in war and the chase, and he could aid the dead in getting to the "other land."[8] But this notion of his power does not imply a belief in his sole disposal of these things.[9]

Creation of Caddi Ayo

The primitive character of the Hasinai concept of this highest deity is reflected in one of their traditions as to his origin. This

[5]Casañas, Relación, fol. 14.

[6]"They say he created everything"; Espinosa, Chrónica,, p. 423. "They said that he has all power and that from him comes all things, which is recognizing a first cause"; Massanet, "Carta," p. 306.

[7]"They all try to keep him pleased with their doings [cossas] and do not dare in any manner to ridicule him. When they are punished for anything they say it is well, supposing that he does it, and that he knows what is best. They also say that those who are displeased with him [que se enojan con el] he punishes," Casañas, Relación, fol. 14.

[8]Ibid., fols. 16, 19.

[9]Joutel showed himself badly informed when he wrote: "As for the knowledge of God, they did not seem to us to have any fixed notion of Him: It is true, we met some on our way, who, as far as we could judge, believed there was some superior Being, which was above all things, and this they testified by lifting up their hands and eyes to heaven, yet without any manner of concern, as believing that the said exalted Being does not regard at all what is done here below. However, as none of them have any places of worship, ceremonies, or prayers, to denote the divine homage, it may be said of them all, that they have no religion, at least those that we saw." This passage is evidence that Joutel did not understand the Indian ceremonies that he saw and that he did not penetrate the Hasinai country to the Chenesi's village where the main fire temple was. Benjamin F. French, ed. Historical Collections of Louisiana, 1: 150–51.

story is recounted for us by Espinosa, who, it would appear from his language, had heard it frequently.[10] It was as follows: In the beginning of the world there were no men, but there was a woman who had two daughters. Strangely enough, though the creation of their chief deity must be accounted for, no explanation is offered for the origin of these three women. One day when one daughter was lying in her sister's lap having her head cleaned of vermin, she was suddenly frightened by the appearance of Caddaja, the devil, in the form of a gigantic, ferocious man, with horns so high that their tips could not be seen. He attacked her, tore her in pieces with his claws, and devoured her. Meanwhile the sister had climbed to the top of a high tree. When Caddaja spied her there he tried to climb up after her, but failed, so he proceeded to cut the tree down with teeth and claws. It is not explained why he did not knock her from the tree with his horns. To escape, she dropped into a deep pond which was at the foot of the tree, dived under, and came to the surface out of reach. The giant, or devil, in order to catch his prize, now began to dry up the lake by drinking the water, but the maiden gave him the laugh and fled to her mother. Together they went to the spot where the sister had been devoured. Here, in the cup of an acorn, was discovered a drop of blood. It was from the veins of the dead daughter. They covered it over with another acorn cup, took it to the lodge, and put it in a jar in a corner. In the night the mother heard a noise like something gnawing the jar and on investigation found that the blood had "congealed" into a little boy, no longer than a finger. She covered it again and the second night, on hearing the same noise repeated, she found that the boy had grown to the size of a large man. Delighted at the advent of man, perhaps, she made him a bow and arrow. On his asking for his mother, they told him how the Caddaja had eaten her, whereupon he set out to avenge her wrongs. Finding the monster, he hurled him from the end of his bow so far that he never again appeared. Returning to

[10] He writes in the historical sense "Yo les replicaba quado me contaban esto . . . y nunca sabian dar respuesta"; Espinosa, Chrónica,, p. 423.

his grandmother and aunt, he told them that it was not good to remain upon the earth, and thereupon went up with them to Cachao Ayo, or the sky, whence he has ever since been ruling all the world. "This," adds Espinosa, "is the first deity whom they recognize and to whom they offer their worship, fearing that he may punish them for the bad as well as reward them for the good they do."[11]

After the Spaniards came, with their strange utensils and implements, the Hasinais, we are told, entertained the notion that the Spaniards had a special god, who gave them the knives, clothes, and other precious things and that the Hasinai chief God was a different one, who supplied only beans, corn, and other things formerly known to and in use by them.[12]

Other Spirits or Deities

Besides Caddi Ayo, other spirits were called upon for help in the various activities of life. Nature, animate and inanimate, was personified, and life was a continual struggle to keep these mysterious personalities favorably disposed. Before going to war, "prayer" was addressed to fire, air, water, and arrows; water was asked to drown, fire to burn, arrows to kill, and wind to carry away their enemies.[13] On the eve of a deer hunt an elaborate ceremonial was performed over the head and horns of a buck, and when one was killed he must not be eaten until some mysterious message had been whispered in his ear.[14] Ceremonies were performed to propitiate the spirits of snakes that they might not kill, and to maize, that it might

[11] Ibid., pp. 423–24. note the parallel between the story of the birth of Caddi Ayo and the Menomini story of the birth of Manabush. Walter J. Hoffman, "The Menomini Indians," in *Fourteenth Annual Report* of the Bureau of American Ethnology (1896) pt. 1, pp. 113–14.

[12] Damián Massanet, "Informe," June 24, 1693, summarized in Dictaman Fiscal, AGN, Historia, vol. 27, fol. 186. It seems that Massanet was drawing largely from Casañas for his information.

[13] Casañas, Relación, fol. 6.

[14] Espinosa, *Chrónica*,, p. 431.

permit itself to be eaten.[15] The prominence of the four cardinal points in many of their ceremonies suggests a personification of even the East, the West, the North, and the South.[16] Death, the hills, the very ground, were of embodied spirits. When a person died they said Death was angry, and they hung on a stake before the house some propitiatory offering. If a dwelling burned, they said the soil or the hill nearby was offended, demanding the house to appease the wrath; and they did not rebuild on the same spot.[17]

Fire played a large part in their religious ceremonial, and Espinosa thought they practiced fire worship, regarding fire as one of the creators.

> With respect to fire, they have extraordinary superstitions. For this there is a special edifice, in which there is a perpetual fire . . . . They say that if it goes out all must die . . . . They have great fear lest fire should be angry, and they give it as tribute the earliest tobacco, the first maize, the first game they kill, and the first fruits of all their harvests. They assert that fire created them, although they are deluded, and they say also that men came out of the sea and scattered themselves over the earth. These two creatures, Water and Fire, they call Nai Cadi. But in all their ceremonies they resort to fire.[18]

Ideas—Creation and the Universe

We have recounted one of their traditions as to the origin of Caddi Ayo, their chief deity, and have seen that they some-

---

[15] Casañas, Relación, fol. 4.

[16] Massanet, "Carta," p. 306; Casañas, Relación, fol. 15.

[17] Ibid., fol. 21.

[18] Espinosa, Chrónica,, pp. 424–25. Casañas, in describing their chief temple, took less note of the fire and emphasized more the coninisi and the deception of the chief priest, who received the gifts. Casañas, Relación, fols. 24–26. See also Fray Francisco Hidalgo to Fray Pedro Mesquia, October 6, 1716. in "Autos sobre diferentes noticias que se han Participado a Su Exa de las entradas que en estos dominios hasen los Franseses por la parte de Coahuila y Providencias dadas para evitarselas y fundacion de la Micion en la Provincia de los Tejas," 1715–18, AGN, Provincias Internas, vol. 181, fols. 484–86.

times attributed the creation of mankind to fire and sometimes to water. There was a tradition, too, that their race sprang directly from animals, some claiming to be descended from bears, others from dogs, or from otters, coyotes, or foxes. They explained this by saying that in the beginning of the world there were many gigantic, horrible demons or ghosts who injured and killed the ancestors of the Hasinais. Therefore to escape destruction, the ancestors transformed themselves into animals, although they yet remained rational men, women, and children, as before.[19]

No less childish was their explanation—one said on good authority to have been common—of the creation of heavens and of the mysteries of the great forces of nature. They said, according to one version, that their ancestors (*los viejos*) themselves made the heavens but that a woman born in an acorn gave them the plan, which was to set stakes in a circle. The acorn woman's functions did not cease there, however, for she continued to sit in the sky and daily to give birth to the sun and moon, as well as to the water when it rained, to the cold, the snow, thunder and lightning, and even maize.[20]

Another version of the way in which their ancestors created the heavens is given by Massanet, in a letter of June 24, 1693. He says they believed "that to do this they built a very high hill beyond the Cadodachos, and that from this hill they put half of the earth above, making the sky (*cielo*), and that there they plant corn and all the other crops," just as they do on earth.[21]

Ideas of a Future Life

"That the Indian believes in a future life his mortuary rites abundantly testify. It may be confidently stated that no tribe of American Indians was without some idea of a life after death;

[19] Espinosa, *Chrónica*, p. 425.
[20] Casañas, Relación, fol. 20.
[21] Massanet, "Informe," 1693, fols. 186–87.

but as to its exact nature and whereabouts the Indians' ideas, differing in different tribes, were vague."[22] The Hasinais were no exception to this rule. Said Espinosa, "These Indians possess much light concerning the immortality of the soul, and they assert it. This belief is evident in their burials and their funeral honors."[23] Both he and Casañas give some indication of the nature of this belief, although they differ much in details, and both leave much to be desired in their accounts. How much they misunderstood, or how much of their own ideas they read into what they saw and heard, we cannot say, but we know that both were highly intelligent witnesses and wrote from intimate personal knowledge.

Casañas gives us our first definite statement as to the nature of this belief in a future life. If he is correct, they had an interesting notion of a temporary stage between death and a permanent future life. According to him they said that when one died, his spirit, which they called *cayo*,[24] went to "another house," kept by a man with great keys larger than oxen. There he awaited his friends until all should be assembled, when they would go to "another land" to settle anew.[25] "For this reason," says our informant, "they bury each one with all his personal possessions and for several days after burial carry him food."[26]

[22] Henry W. Henshaw, "Popular Fallacies Respecting the Indians," *American Anthropologist* 7 (January–March, 1905): 108–109. For information on the mortuary rites of different tribes as illustrating this point, see H. C. Yarrow, "A Further Contribution to the Study of Mortuary Customs of the North American Indians," in *First Annual Report* of the Bureau of American Ethnology (1881).

[23] Espinósa, *Chrónica,*, p. 425.

[24] Casañas rendered this "soul" (*alma*). Relación, fol. 18.

[25] "Quando uno muere se ba su alma q ho la ygnoran que en su ydioma llaman Cayo, va a otra Cassa donde los aguarda un hombre que esten todos Juntos; y este es uno q dicen tiene unas grandes llabes; y dizen que son mas grandes q los Bueyez que tenemos aca, y estando todos Juntos han de yr, a otra tierra a poblar denuebo." Casañas, Relación, fol. 18.

[26] Massanet said that they believed that both the body and the soul went to the "other land." Massanet," Informe," fol. 186.

Unlike Casañas, Espinosa does not record a belief in the waiting place between death and the journey to the "other land," but he ascribes to them a belief in a place of punishment, which, however, is reserved mainly for enemies. He writes:

They say that as soon as the spirits leave the bodies, they journey at once to a place in the west, then ascend into the air, and pass near by the place of the Great Chief, whom they call Caddi Ayo. From here they go to stop at a house, situated in the south, which, they say, is the house of Death. And what will death be but eternity? [27]

Of the nature of existence there, he says:

They imagine, or their old men [28] persuade them, that they all will be happy, suffering no hunger, sickness, or other troubles. They think that all will remain in the condition in which death took them; thus, if a woman died pregnant she would always remain so, or if she died with a child at her breast, she would continue carrying it when there. But they do not say that man and wife return to married life. I inquired with care if all go to this place without punishment, and they said 'yes, except the bad,' among whom they count their enemies. These go to the House of El Texino, who is the Devil, and who, when they are there, punishes them soundly. They do not consider deserving of Inferno adulterers, sodomites, fornicators, or thieves, for they recognize only visible wrong, like bodily injury. [29] And thus when they die, all are buried with the pretended conjurations of their priests who say the dead are going to their rest, and that the wrong they have done is erased, but that unless they pray for them the Devil takes them in his house. [30]

The view just set forth does not exactly tally with Henshaw's assertion that "The American Indian seems not to have evolved the idea of hell and future punishment." [31] Evidently

[27] Massanet, quite to the contrary, said that they believed that toward the sunrise was the road by which they must go to the sky. Ibid.

[28] Priests, no doubt.

[29] "Solo concibe maldad sensible, en quanto al coporal agravio."

[30] Espinosa, Chrónica, pp. 425–26.

[31] Henshaw, "Popular Fallacies," American Anthropologist 7 (January–March, 1905): 109.

the Hasinais believed that their enemies and such of them as neglected the proper observance of priestly rites would be assigned in the hereafter to a different place from that to which "good" Indians were expected to go. In this connection it may not be amiss to cite a parallel belief among the Wichitas, relatives of the Hasinais. Athanase de Mézières, one of the best-informed Indian agents of the eighteenth century, after long experience among the various tribes of Texas and Louisiana, in 1772 made a visit to the Taovayas [Wichitas] on the Red River and while there made a report upon their habits. Speaking of their religion he says:

They firmly believe in the reality of another life, in which the good (in whose front ranks will be the warriors), will be rewarded and removed to a certain country where they will enjoy perpetual youth and strength, crystalline waters, exquisite fruits, and other delicacies known to them in this world. On the contrary the bad will be forever cast out among briars and rocks, surrounded by poisonous snakes, and exposed to thirst, hunger, disease, and the worst calamities thinkable.[32]

In a later report [1778], made as a result of a second visit to their villages, he said the Taovayas believed that their desserts in the next world would depend upon their exploits in this one.[33]

The Coninisi

Besides the care of the fire in the main temple, the Chenesi was specifically charged with the custody and consultation of the two boys, called the *coninisi*, or *coninisis*, who acted as intermediaries between the Gran Chenesi and Caddi Ayo. Belief in the fiction of these coninisi is perhaps the most remarkable feature of the religious life of the Hasinais. Concerning them Casañas and Espinosa, both eyewitnesses, give testi-

[32] Athanase de Mézières to the Baron de Ripperdá, July 4, 1772, AGN, Historia, vol. 51, fol. 33.
[33] Mézières to Teodoro de Crois, April 18, 1778, AGN, Historia, vol. 28, fol. 277.

mony which is in essential agreement. It was taught that they had been sent from Cachao Ayo, or the sky, by the great chief above. Different explanations were given to the Spaniards why they could not be seen, one being that if any person should see them he would die; but more commonly it was stated that though formerly they had been visible, they had been burned with the house where they were kept and had gone up in the smoke, leaving only their spirits. But stories differed as to the time when this ascent occurred, and they seem to have been designed to satisfy the curious. Casañas heard this explanation as early as 1691, while Espinosa was told that it occurred about 1714, when the Yojuanes burned the temple and other buildings.[34]

The coninisi were kept in a house distinct from the main temple. It appears that formerly there had been only one coni-nisi house, for Casañas explicitly describes one structure as "the house of the coninisi," but in Espinosa's time there were two, and it may be that the additional one was made during the rebuilding which took place in 1716 after the Yojuane raid. Indeed it is not certain that the house of the coninisi described by Casañas is not the main fire temple described by Espinosa, or rather, its predecessor. If this be true, the separate houses were a specialization that occurred after his day.[35] The single building described by Casañas was larger than the house in which the Great Chenesi then lived, while the two struc-tures described by Espinosa were small ones, standing a gun-shot from the main Fire House.[36]

The apparatus used in the cult is not without interest to the general reader, while to the investigator it may serve as a clue to the inner meaning of some of the practices. Espinosa tells us that in one of these houses there were "two small chests [petaquillas] about three-fourths [of a vara long] with painted and carefully made reed covers and sitting upon a sort of

[34]Casañas, Relación, fols. 24, 27–28; Espinosa, Chrónica, pp. 424–25.
[35]Casañas, Relación, fol. 14.
[36]Ibid.

wooden altar built on four small forked poles." With another religious, he says,

I examined and found the chests to contain inside four or five porringer-shaped dishes or vases of black wood, all carefully made, with four feet, some representing little ducks, with both head and tail, and others with the head, tail, and feet of a crocodile or lizard. Besides this there were feathers of all sizes and colors, some bunches of turkey feathers, loose white breast feathers and bundles of tuft feathers. Coronas of skins and plumes, and virrete of the same, with many little crane's bones, which serve as flutes or fifes, and others of carved reeds, with appropriate holes, together with many other little instruments they use in their mitotes or dances. That one of these little houses containing the two little chests is very well swept.[37]

Consulting the Coninisi

Casañas gives a graphic description of the ceremony of consulting the coninisi, which he calls "talking with God." The people having assembled at the coninisi temple, the caddis and elders entered it naked, the rest of the people remaining outside. Inside was a fire that was always kept burning by youthful servants, except during a part of the ceremony. The contrivance in which the coninisi, or their spirits, were kept was described as "a round stick like the top of a candy box; it is inside a skin covering like pigskin; around the box are placed some morsels of what the Indians carry as offerings; in the middle it is deep; here is placed tobacco that the boys may make."[38] This contrivance was placed on a table or platform

---

[37]Espinosa, Chrónica, pp. 424–25; copied by Fray Juan Agustín Morfí, "Historia de Texas," trans. F. F. Hilder, MS no. 1750 in National Anthropological Archives, Smithsonian Institution, bk. 3, pp. 72–73; also described by Casañas, Relación, fol. 15.

[38]Casañas, Relación, fol. 16: ". . . un palo redondo a modo de una cubierta de caxita de dulzie; y esta dentro de una cubierta de pellejo, como pergamina, por Rededor de la Caxita tenia puesto algunas Migagitas de lo que los Yndios le llevan a ofreser, al medio esta honda aqui pone tobaco . . . para q los dos ninos chuparan."

about two varas high and on each side of the platform were two reed trunks or hampers having orifices. It is probable that they are the same ones as those described by Espinosa. Into these trunks, Casañas thought, the Chenesi dropped the offerings brought by the persons assembled. Going to the fire he took live coals with a broken dish and with them burned incense of tobacco and the fat of buffalo heart. This done, he put out the fire, leaving the room dark, and while those outside were dancing and singing he proceeded to talk with the coninisi. As Casañas understood it, in his natural voice the Chenesi would tell the boys what they should say to God, promising that all the Hasinais would mend their ways if he would give them good harvests, plentiful game, etc. The instructions over he would take a little calabash filled with rattling *quentas*. Sometimes he threw it upon the ground, explaining that God was angry and refused to talk. Thereupon the frightened assembly would cry out earnest promises. The promises secured, the Chenesi would raise the calabash and, in a feigned boy's voice, report God's approval and then repeat it in his natural voice to the company. Upon being dismissed, says Casañas, those assembled would rush out "like kids from a corral." [39] Casañas accused the Chenesi of using this ceremony to frighten his subjects into making him plentiful gifts. He tried, also, by argument and ridicule, to do away with the abuse, but the Chenesi, though he did not receive Christian baptism at the padre's hands, said that he and his people greatly loved the coninisi and would not give them up. [40]

The Main Fire Temple

The central shrine of the Hasinai cult was the temple already mentioned as presided over by the Great Chenesi. It was called by the natives the house of the Great Chief or Caddi Ayo, and by the Spaniards the Fire House. It seems that this

[39] Casañas, Relación, fols. 15–16.
[40] Ibid., fols. 15–16, 22.

Fire House is what Casañas designated as the Chenesi's house. About 1714, it appears, the Yojuanes destroyed it and its appurtenances, which may account for some differences between the reports of Casañas and Espinosa. The Fire House that was rebuilt in 1716 Espinosa described as round, large, and thatched with grass. In other words, it was constructed essentially like the dwellings. It was located between the Neche and the Hainai.[41]

The furniture of this temple was thus described:

It contains, inside, a canopy made of mats; in the bed-nook are three mats, two of them very small; and on one side of the door on benches there are other mats rolled up. Before the bed is a small, square, four-legged bench, made of a single piece and raised somewhat above the earth. On the benches are kept tobacco and a pipe with plumes, and large earthen pots, resembling censers, which they supply with fat and tobacco. The fire or blaze they always make of four very large and heavy trunks, pointing in the four cardinal directions. The kindling wood is very fine and is kept in stacks outside.

Espinosa adds, "Here gather the elders for their consultations and dances preparatory of war and when there is a dearth of water for their crops."[42]

A similar temple seems to have been at the Kadohadacho village south of the Red River. About half of a league south of the caddi's house Terán saw, on a hill overlooking the whole country, a "temple in which they worshipped and made offerings to their gods," and which, according to the record, was little different from the caddi's house.[43]

For the subgroups of the confederacy there were local fire temples, if not one for each tribe. says Espinosa:

[41] Espinosa, *Chrónica*, p. 423; Morfí, "Historia," 3: 71.

[42] Espinosa, *Chrónica*, p. 424. That this temple contained a pipe with plumes indicates that it may have been the assembly house where Joutel smoked.

[43] This may be the famous hill that all Caddos regarded as their primitive house. Domingo de Terán, "Descripción y Diaria Demarcación," 1691, AGN, Historia, vol. 27, fol. 33.

the [main] Fire House is that of the Ainais. It is like a parish church or a cathedral. There is another at the Naichas and still others at the Nacocdochis and the Nasonis. From this one [of the Ainais] fire is carried to these other houses. To hold their special festivals of the year it is customary for the Naichas and Ainais to meet at the same temple and the Nacodochis and Nazonis in the other. All the houses, or most of them, supply themselves with fire from the principal house. Not that they carry it from there every day, but that when they build them they carry it from there and preserve it. If by chance it goes out they consider it an omen that all the family must die; and they carry it again from the temple house with many ceremonies, which I shall describe in their proper place.[44]

Mortuary Customs

Much light on the religious ideas of the Hasinais, particularly their notions of a hereafter, can be gathered from their mortuary customs. Casañas gives us detailed information on this subject, particularly relative to the burial of leading personages. As there was an epidemic during his residence there, and as he made special efforts to eradicate some of the customs he saw, he speaks with no little authority. Espinosa, who wrote after a long residence among the Hasinais, also gives us specific information on the subject.

The Hasinais seem uniformly to have observed the practice of inhumation within less than two days after death, except in case of the Chenesi.[45] Their funerals were the occasion of much lamentation and of elaborate ceremonies performed by

[44] Espinósa, Chrónica,, p. 425.

[45] Casañas, Relación, fol. 34. Espinosa says they kept the dead some hours; Chrónica, p. 425. Macarty, in arguing that the Hasinais did not dominate all the tribes "a hundred leagues in every direction," called attention to the fact that "some burn the dead, others bury them, and the greater part of them leave them in the open field." He evidently included a wide range of tribes in this view. Chevalier Barthélemy de Macarty to Don Ángel de Martos y Navarrete, Natchitoches, November 17, 1763, Nacogdoches Archives, Austin, Texas. A typed copy can be found among the Bolton Papers, Bancroft Library.

priests charged with this particular function. Coffins were used, and the dead were carried to the grave on biers. A man's bow and arrows and other personal property were interred with him for use in the other country; and, likewise, with a woman were buried her baskets, grinding implements, and clay vessels. The excavation of a grave at Atlanta, Texas, in the Caddo country, gives ground for thinking that after the coming of the horse, the warrior's steed was buried with him. When the funeral party was on the way to the grave, arrows were shot toward the sky to inform the keeper of the "other house" of the approach of the deceased. The food was offered the dead and kept for a time on his grave that he might have strength to reach his destination. Before burying the body, it was washed and dressed in its best garments.[46]

Casañas thus described, as he understood it, the funeral of a leading personage, not the Chenesi. To witness or take part in the ceremonies, the chief men were all present. To conduct them there were three priests, two of whom, naked, began with a performance over the empty coffin. Walking about it and striking attitudes over it, mumbling vigorously the while, they put upon the coffin tobacco, an herb called *acoxio,* and bows and arrows. These exertions were so vigorous that, although the weather was cold, they caused the priests to perspire. Next was the preparation of the grave, which for a leading man was always near the house. Going to the spot, the two priests again repeated some words and with a pick struck a blow first at the head and then at the foot of the grave before the diggers were allowed to begin their work. While the grave was being dug the priests returned to the dwelling, ordered the dead put into the coffin, and after talking to it for a time as to a living person, they went aside to deliver "to God" a message for the deceased. Some time having been spent in talking thus, they brought the answer to the corpse.

Next, what seems to have been an eulogy was pronounced

[46]Casañas, Relación, fols. 18, 20–22; Espinosa, Chrónica, pp. 425–26.

by a third and older priest, who stood in the midst of the assembly, armed with some weapon,[47] and for an hour recounted the deeds of the deceased in war and the chase, estimated his friends' loss at this death, and exhorted them all to weep for him. This discourse over, he sat down by the dead man, repeated the substance of his eulogy and entreated him to wait for them all to join him at the "other house," when they would go together to the other land.

The coffin was now put upon a bier and carried to the grave, arrows being shot on the way, according to the custom, to notify the keeper of the other house of the dead man's coming. All his personal belongings were carried to the grave, deposited at the bottom, and the coffin placed upon them. While the grave was being filled, amid the lamentations of friends, the two priests talked again, asking that the corpse, which was weak at death, might be allowed to eat the food supplied, to give it strength to reach the "other house." When the company dispersed, food, water, tobacco, and fire were brought and put upon the grave. Food was frequently carried for some days, and it seems that a special functionary was kept there or was frequently sent to intercede for the dead.[48] Some claimed they had even seen a dead man eat the food thus left for him. When one of Joutel's party died at the Kadohadacho village, a chief's wife carried food to the grave, a fact indicating that in this respect they had the same custom as the Hasinais.[49]

"These," said Casañas, "are the ceremonies they perform when one of the principal men dies. When a private individual passes on they are the same, only there is less pomp."[50]

From the pen of Espinosa we have the following description

[47]Casañas says that he was armed with one of the best weapons they have, and that twice he saw him bear a sword (sin guarnición) during the ceremony.

[48]"Y ay unos tienen por oficio de yr encima de la sepultura poniendose a hablar alli solos." Casañas Relación, fols. 18, 20–22.

[49]Margry, ed. and trans., Découvertes, 3: 406.

[50]Casañas, Relación, fol. 22.

of the mortuary ceremonies performed when one died in war
or away from home:

Having provided a quantity of the food of the season they invite all
the people to assemble on a certain day. About a stone's throw from
the house they erect a pyramid of fine wood. The men and women
all together cast themselves upon their beds, weeping, with hair
much disheveled. A chief of the priests (*Santones*) enters and speaks
a few words to them and then begins a flood of tears, or we might
better say, an *ahullido a que corresponden las mugeres todas planidoras*.
Then as many as seven men go out of the house, and, turning their
faces to the east and having in front of them a little vessel with
moistened ground corn, they make their prayers. The conjuration by
the chief priest ended, they take from the vessel a part of the moist
corn and scatter it to the four winds. The remainder is eaten by
three of them, who serve as sponsors of the funeral. When the seven
return inside, the mourners renew their clamor. The chief men seat
themselves in their order, the sponsors sitting with the mourners,
and offer to an old priest tobacco and cornflour. Accepting it, he
turns to the fire, which is in the middle of the house, prays his
falsehood, throws some of the tobacco and flour into the fire, and
then returns the rest to the sponsors. This over, two or three Indians
step out and give a bow and arrow to the wife or mother of the
deceased. Then, beginning with the captains, one by one, each in
turn offers to the mourners six or eight arrows according to his grief.
Next the women offer condolence and contribute their strings of
beads, knives, or clothing. Of all these things together, adding good
deer skins, and all the treasures of the deceased, they make up his
bundle, rolling it in a mat. Meanwhile an old man and a younger
one are singing in doleful strains. One of the sponsors shoulders the
bundle, another takes fire, another a handful of dry grass, and, going
to the pyramid, they set it afire on all sides, burning to ashes the mat
with all its arrows and clothing. Meanwhile, the confusion made by
the cries of the mourners and friends is doubled by means of bells
while others in the crowd are laughing and making merry. The ceremony is crowned by a feast which they provide for all. When this is
over the company breaks up. They say all this is done so that the
soul of the deceased may go to the house of rest, or so that when he
comes to see his body he will perceive what has been done for him.[51]

[51]Espinosa, *Chrónica*, pp. 426.

The Chenesi's Funeral

It happened that while Casañas was among the Hasinais he saw the preparation for the burial of the Great Chenesi. What he says of them not only adds to our knowledge of their mortuary customs, but also reflects the exalted position of this dignitary.

The Chenesi's funeral was more elaborate than that of any other personage. His body was kept for two days in order that all the tribes might send embassies to take part in the burial ceremonies.[52] After performing the usual rites attending the death of a principal man, the Chenesi's body was buried in a large coffin. For many days after the interment, postinhumation ceremonies were enacted. One feature of them consisted of dancing for ten days and nights before what, to Casañas, was a representation of the earth and the "moons." What he called the earth was a large ball of grass set on the point of a high pole in front of the Chenesi's door. The "moons" were represented by setting poles in a circle, presumably with other figures upon them.[53]

I have not seen all of this," says one witness, "but I have seen all the tribes gathered to perform these ceremonies, and I have seen all of these insignia. I saw the coffin, which was as large as a *carro*. But God willed that the Chenesi when at the point of death should ask to be made a Christian, and I had him confess the mysteries of our holy faith, baptizing him on his bed in the presence of many Indians, and before whom he was destined to be preserved as Chenesi.

[52] "Porque todas las nuebe Naciones q. tiene todas hazen estas ceremonias," Casañas, Relación, fol. 22. That they came to the Chenesi's house instead of performing ceremonies in their own villages is made evident below.

[53] The above is what seem to be the meaning of a very obscure passage in Casañas's account. His words are, in part, as follows: "Hazen otras Ceremonias semejantes a estas, y otras, como ponerle el mundo delantte de la puertta q. lo forman plantando una Asta mui alta, y en la puntta una bola grande de zacatte, le ponen las lunas, a senalandolas con unos palos altos formando una, o delante de todo esto vailan diez dias, y diez noches." Relación, fol. 22.

All were very much pleased . . . . The great Chenesi's recovery of entire health has been the confusion of all [enemies].[54]

One may be pardoned, perhaps, for regretting that this unexpected recovery deprived us of additional information on the subject of the Chenesi's funeral.

So tenaciously did they adhere to their own burial customs that the missionaries could not, for some time at least, obtain permission to take the dead bodies of baptized Hasinais to the mission church. One attempt to do so on the part of Fray Miguel Font Cuberta, nearly caused an uprising against the missionaries.[55]

The funeral of the head civil chief, as well as that of the Chenesi, seems to have been very elaborate, for Espinosa tells us that eight days were consumed in the burial of two successive head chiefs who died at the same time about 1716.[56]

Divination and Astrology

A religion which embraced a belief in myriad spirits and occult forces naturally fostered primitive faith in signs and in superstitious practices designed to give light on future events or to facilitate communication with unseen powers. Among the Hasinais, to meet, while hunting or on the war path, a large flock of birds, which they called *banit*, was considered a sure sign that absent ones were nearby and approaching. Important ceremonials were set by the movements of the constellations, and we are told that the medicine men were "graduates" in astrology.[57] Future events were predicted by means of a contrivance made of a fox's tail, while in a certain ceremony, an *Ygui*, or eagle, whose wing was "possessed" and properly conjured, was supposed to assist in prediction. A more common means of prognostication was for a priest or

[54] Ibid.
[55] Ibid.
[56] Espinosa, *Chrónica*, p. 441.
[57] Ibid., pp. 429, 432.

other functionary to put himself into a trance or stupor by means of herb concoctions and, upon recovery, to relate what he had seen. We have already mentioned this method of locating an enemy or predicting the outcome of a campaign. In the performance of religious rites frequent use was made also of tobacco and the fat of buffalo heart. [Fray Antonio] Olivares tells of a use in their religious rites of a drink called peyote, which caused "seeing visions and phantoms," [58] and Espinosa tells of a drink of boiled wild olives (*azebuche*) similarly used.

Periodical Ceremonial

Every important event in the life of the Hasinais, as was the case with the Indians generally, was attended by more or less elaborate ceremonies of a religious and social significance. Because of their religious element, the priests and medicine men played an important part in them; and because of their social significance they frequently involved sports and contests, and usually a good deal of feasting. Aside from those ceremonials that we have already incidentally described in connection with war, the chase, and funerals, the most important were those connected with the prophecy of the seasons, the planting of crops, the gathering of the harvest, and the pledging of friendship.

Prophecy of the Seasons

Connected with the agricultural life of the people there were three classes of ceremonies. The first was that connected with the prognostication of the forthcoming season. It was held in the moon of Sacabbi, or February, just before the planting season. The whole tribe assembled on a given day, bringing an abundant supply of food, and on the next day the function began. In it the medicine men rather than the priests were the

[58] Ibid., pp. 430, 432; Fray Antonio Olivares, quoted in Dictamen Fiscal, AGN, Historia, vol. 27, fol. 194.

A Wichita grass lodge under construction. Photograph taken by James Mooney at the Trans-Mississippi and International Exposition, Omaha, Nebraska, 1898. This lodge is similar to those described by European chroniclers of the Hasinais. Courtesy National Anthropological Archives (neg. no. 34,729-A), Smithsonian Institution.

masters of ceremonies. Two or three of them spent the morning in purifying the *casina,* made of boiled laurel leaves, and the old men of the *mesta* take their drinks. Later, facing the posts of the lodge round which the ceremony was held, they muttered some kind of mummery. With an eagle's wing in hand they now danced, meanwhile saluting the fire and throwing upon it powdered tobacco, while a pipe was passed from mouth to mouth. Then followed a pantomime signifying, as Espinosa understood it, that the eagle whose wings were being used was going up to consult the great chief concerning the forecast of the year. Now, says Espinosa, "The old men having made their almanac privately and between their teeth, come forth to declare it, or divulge it to the public, saying for example that this year will be abundant in nuts and acorns but not in corn. In the years when there are many insects they say there will be a large crop of beans."[59]

Planting Ceremonies

Before beginning to plant in the spring a special ceremony, apparently designed to assure a bountiful harvest, was performed. It was participated in by the women alone, since they were the planters. On a certain day, prearranged, they gathered, young and old (evidently the young married women were excluded), bringing a supply of food, while an old woman, mistress of the ceremony, brought a quantity of thin reed bark. From this bark the assembled women made two or three mats and gave them to a personage, probably a priest, who carried them, as an offering, to the Fire House. The ceremony was ended by feasting. It is not clear whether the adz-making and ground-clearing by men and women near the village Fire House, as described by Espinosa, was a mere symbolic ceremonial or was the performance of the actual task of clearing, as described by Joutel, but Espinosa seems to consider it a preliminary planting ceremonial.[60]

Harvest Ceremonial

The harvest or the acquisition of any important supply of food was attended by ceremonials regarded by our witness as in the nature of blessings or thanksgivings, some of which were participated in by a household or village, others by several tribes. Massanet tells us that, "They observed the custom never to taste any food without first taking a portion of it to their minister for sacrifice; they did this with the produce of their lands, such as corn, beans, watermelons, and calabashes, as well as

[59] Espinosa, Chrónica, p. 430.
[60] Ibid., p. 431.

with the buffalo meat obtained by hunting." Even the partaking of a meal, if of unusual significance, might be preceded by such a performance.[61] Espinosa tells us that of the first cutting of tobacco a tamma gathered a portion and delivered it to the priest especially charged with blessing the harvest. In these ceremonies blowing to the four winds the smoke of tobacco and buffalo fat seems to have been a prominent feature.

New Corn Ceremony

With respect to new corn it was believed that if any one ate of it before it had received the proper blessing he would be bitten by snakes. The new corn ceremony was described by Joutel, Casañas, and Espinosa, with some differences of emphasis and interpretation, but with substantial agreement as to its essential features. Joutel's version of it as performed at a Nasoni chief's house is as follows:

> When the Indian corn began to ripen, I noted a ceremony performed at the said cabin by one of the elders who came there. Upon his arrival the women picked a large number of ears of corn, parched them, and put them in a hamper, which they placed upon the ceremonial stool that served for this purpose only. . . . When all was arranged the elder approached the stool, accompanied by the head of the cabin, and there they remained a good hour and a half, muttering over the ears [of corn], after which they distributed it to the women, who gave it to the youth, and also presented some of it to us. But neither the elder nor the chief of the cabin ate of it.

When he asked the reason for this abstinence, Joutel understood his host to say that he would not eat the new corn until eight days had passed—"eight days," of course, meaning a week. The rest of the community, however, began at once to eat it. Strangely enough, Espinosa, whose description agrees with this in the main, makes the eating of the corn by the priest a prominent part of the ceremony.[62]

[61] Massanet, "Carta," p. 306.
[62] Margry, ed. and trans., *Découvertes*, 3: 401; French, ed., *Historical Collections*, 1: 151; Espinósa, *Chrónica*, p. 431.

The September Festival

The most notable tribal festival of the year, attended by the largest concourse of people, was that held after the harvests, during the crescent September noon. Notice of it was sent out to the families several days ahead, and preparation was made by the officials. Six days in advance numerous hunters met outside one of the temples. After a ceremony performed inside by the older priests, the Chenesi or some other dignitary of rank came out and ordered the hunters to go out in all directions to hunt for deer, while he and his associates continued their prayers to Caddi Ayo, predicting that they would be successful. When the six days hunt was over, all the deer killed were brought to the temple, and the flesh, except the head and entrails, was prepared for the feast. On the afternoon before the opening ceremony, the people gathered round the temple, dressed in their holiday attire.

Early in the night (*prima noche*) while the families were ranged round their fires outside, the priests, medicine men, and chief met in the temple and for an hour performed elaborate ceremonies, consisting of petitions to Caddi Ayo, throwing particles of food into the fire, drinking a concoction of boiled wild olive and by turns blowing smoke into the fire, above, to the earth, and to the four winds.

As midnight approached, "cerca de Galicanto," while rattles of gourds were being played to keep the populace awake, a crier began to call for offerings, family by family. Three by three the women, one from each house, entered the temple bearing jars of flour or baked loaves, which were deposited by functionaries in two large baskets. This over, the offerings were distributed among the leading men inside.

After midnight a sentinel was placed to give notice when the constellation of the kids [Capricorn], called by them the Women, should be directly above the temple. At the signal from the sentinel the Chenesi or some other principal priest went outside with a companion to a circle made of green reeds set in the earth round a large fire constantly fed with fuels. Seating themselves within the circle, these priests were followed by the women and girls who ranged themselves in files according to their age or condition. Now from a bowery east of the circle and containing a fire, there emerged three old men gaily dressed. As they slowly approached the circle, with pauses between steps, the priests and the women within the circle sang or chanted. As the three entered the circle the singing stopped and the first old man began a speech or recital in a high voice, "without saying anything reasonable." This finished, the women, still seated, each held forth a little jar of flour or bread, the singing was resumed, the old men retired in silence, and hurrying young men stacked the offerings outside the circle.

About an hour afterward this ceremony was repeated, apparently only once, but the two old men and the women, accompanied by gourd rattlers, continued their singing, with some pauses, until sunrise. Then the singing ceased, and young men went into the woods shouting, apparently to the sun, and at the first ray they rushed out "with huzzas." Our informant evidently had no definite notion of the meaning of this part of the ceremony, for he says: "It appears that either they give it [the sun] thanks for the past harvest, or invite it to be present at the footrace which begins at once." The race was run upon a course that extended to and from a tree about a musket shot away and was participated in by men, boys, and even girls, grouped according to their sizes. The victors were applauded, and the laggards pitied or jeered.

The running over, a dance was performed by the whole concourse. The men and women faced each other, in pairs, in a circle, and when dancing, did not move from their places. They were accompanied by the noise of rattles, some twenty singers, and a drum made of a hollow log set in the ground and beaten by eight men with clubs. This dance, which lasted till noon, ended with ceremonials.[63]

---

[63] Ibid., pp. 431–33.

The Calumet

There is plenty of evidence to show that the calumet cere-mony was regularly performed by the Hasinais, although it seems to have escaped students hitherto and although there are no elaborate descriptions of its details.[64]

According to Penicaut, when St. Denis arrived in 1714 at one of the Hasinai villages (evidently that of the Hainais, since the woman Angelina was there) "they chanted . . . their calumet of peace, which lasted three days."[65] Domingo Ramón, who in 1716 was met by twenty-five principal Hasinais, five leagues east of the Trinity [River] on the highway to the Nabedaches, thus describes his reception:

Embracing me with especial joy and satisfaction, they sat down on the blankets [gergas, furnished by Ramón] brought forth a large pipe, which they use only for peace, took out some of their tobacco, of which they have much, filled the pipe and put a coal in the middle. The captains smoked first, in this fashion: they blew the first puff toward the sky, the second to the east, the third to the west, the fourth to the north, the fifth to the south, and the sixth toward the earth, these being the signs of true peace. The pipe is decorated with many white feathers covering the stem, which is more than a *vara* long from one end to the other. They gave it to me to smoke in the same way, I making the same sign of peace. In turn they gave it to everybody, even the women. The chiefs took tobacco out of their pouches, made a heap in their midst, and filled the pipe from that. I did the same, giving them some of my tobacco.

Espinosa, who participated in this ceremony, said the pipe was bronze.[66] Espinosa tells us that Governor Alarcón was met in 1718 near the Hainai mission by the Indians, who bathed his face "and gave him the pipe of peace." In 1719 while La Harpe was at the Kadohadacho village, the Nadaco chiefs vis-

[64] Hodge, ed., *Handbook* 1: 195.
[65] Margry, ed. and trans., *Découvertes*, 5: 500.
[66] Ramón, "Derrotero," 1716, AGN, *Historia*, vol. 27, fol. 155; See Espinosa, Diario, June 29, 1716, AGN, *Historia*, vol. 394.

ited him and four times chanted the calumet with him.[67] In 1721 while Aguayo was near the Nabedache village, he was received by the "signs of peace, which is for all to use the same pipe, mixing their tobacco with ours."[68]

Thus we find ample evidence that among the Hasinai branch of the Caddos the calumet was in common use. Turning to the Red River Caddos we find similar evidences of its use there. In 1719 La Harpe was received at the Kadahadacho village by the pipe ceremony, participated in by the Kadahadachos, Natsoos, Natchitoches, and Nassonites. He says, "the four nations chanted me the calumet, which is a mark of alliance among these people. This performance lasted twenty-four hours, during which time their music did not stop a minute. If the ceremony is fatiguing, it is not less burdensome to those to whom they render these honors, for they are obliged to make them presents." Two days later they performed the calumet ceremony for Blanc, a war chief of the Natchitoches, who was with La Harpe as a guide.[69]

Medical Practice

The methods of Hasinai doctors, called *connas*, were a combination of rudimentary medical and surgical practice with a free use of charms, incantations, and sorcery. On the one hand, they used in their cure many herbs whose medicinal properties had been discovered through long experience, and we are told that of such things they had extensive and useful knowledge.[70] On the side of surgery, boils, tumors, and other swellings were often treated by scarifying the affected spot with shell, stone, or snake's rattle and then sucking the blood or pus. Wounds were cleansed in the same way, and undesired bleeding was stopped by simples [medicinal herbs]. Sweating

---

[67] Espinosa, *Chrónica*, p. 438; Margry, ed. and trans., *Découvertes*, 6: 275.
[68] Juan de la Peña, Diario, AGN, *Historia*, vol. 28, fol. 35.
[69] Margry, ed. and trans., *Découvertes*, 6: 255, 266, 273.
[70] Espinosa, *Chrónica*, p. 428.

Small pot (natural size) with [concentric] circles, found in a historic grave on the Emma Owens Fa[rm], Ande[rs]on County, Texas. Courtesy Texas Archeological Research l[ab], (neg. [n]o. 41AN21-8), University of Texas, Austin.

was extensively used as a cure. To apply this remedy a fire was placed under the patient's bed, for all the beds were raised, and kept burning for hours, until, as our informant puts it, he was on a very gridiron.[71] We find no trace of the specialized temescal so common in some tribes.

With cures based on sound experience, the medicine men mingled ignorance, sorcery, and trickery. They taught that *aguain*, or disease, consisted of invisible shafts from the bow of

[71] Margry, ed. and trans., *Découvertes*, 3: 383; Espinosa, *Chrónica*, p. 428.

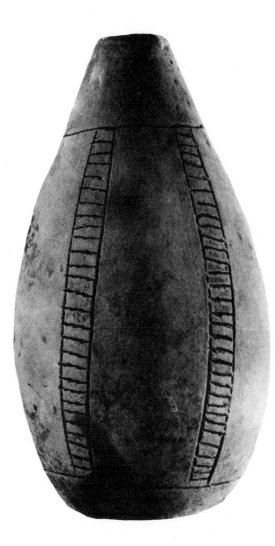

Earthenware bottle (8 × 4½ in.) found on the Jim P. Allen farm, Cherokee County, Texas. This is an excellent illustration of the so-called ladder design. Courtesy Texas Archeological Research Lab (neg. no. 41CE12-39), University of Texas, Austin.

Texino, or the Devil, hurled at mortals through the charms of their enemies. Accordingly, the medicine men of these enemies were sometimes invoked to aid in the cure, in the belief that they would respond by appearing as *tecoletes*, or owls. Hence, to hear an owl hoot during the performance of a cure was a good omen.[72] They taught also that by divination they could determine whether or not a disease was curable while the drinking of bitter herb concoctions by the doctors themselves was regarded as a proper means of helping the patient. One method of combating disease was to drive it out by smoking the affected part with the fumes of buffalo fat and tobacco, or charming it away with strange noises.[73]

Espinosa thus describes procedures accompanying the sweating and sucking process: "To cure a patient they make a large fire" under the bed, and *palillos* "provide flutes and a feather fan. The instruments are manufactured [sticks] with notches resembling a snake's rattle. This palillo placed in a hollow bone upon a skin makes a noise nothing less than devilish. Before touching it they drink their herbs boiled and covered with much foam and begin to perform their dance without moving from one spot, accompanied by the music of Inferno, or the song of the damned, for only in Inferno will the discordant gibberish which the quack sets up find its like. This ceremony lasts from midafternoon to nearly sunrise. The quack interpolates his song by applying his cruel medicaments."[74]

When a *conna* was particularly unfortunate in his medical ministrations the people might turn against him and, we are told by two independent witnesses, sometimes might even kill him.[75] But they had a strong hold upon the people and were

[72] Espinosa, *Chrónica*, p. 428.
[73] Ibid.
[74] Ibid., p. 429; Casañas, Relación, fol. 32.
[75] Casañas, Relacion, fol. 19; Espinosa, *Chrónica*, pp. 428, 429: "Estos Medicos son muy atensididos y respectados de todos, y en su eslimación son los oraculos de sus emboyimientos."

the worst opponents of the Spanish missionaries. It is partly for this reason that the early Spanish observers quite uniformly called them quacks, frauds, and liars and, in their own ignorance, even believed them capable and guilty of witchcraft.

8

War Customs and Ceremonials

War being decided upon, extensive ceremonies were performed for the purpose of inspiring the warriors, training the young in the art of war, and winning the cooperation of super-human forces. During the absence of the war party the women kept up demonstrations and the return of a successful party was the occasion of elaborate victory ceremonies, embracing honors for distinguished warriors, torture for prisoners, and, sometimes, ceremonial cannibalism.

While Joutel's party was among the Hasinais, these tribes prepared for a successful campaign against the Canohatinnos. This gave Joutel an excellent opportunity to observe Hasinai war customs. During the year 1690 and 1691 they were again engaged in war, and as a result Casañas and the Talons added detailed information based upon ocular testimony. At a later date Espinosa and others recorded numerous war customs observed by them. Some of these will be described here, primarily to illustrate their extensive ceremonial.

War Preliminaries

Before going to war the matter was gravely discussed in a council, participated in sometimes by the leading men and even the warriors of many tribes, called together by messengers formally commissioned. If the decision was for war the allies were duly notified. If invited to join in a war, on the other hand, the messenger bringing the invitation was received by the leading men with much ceremony, regaled, and given a seat of honor while the answer was being deliberated upon.[1] War parties raised to go against the Apaches sometimes included bands from an especially large number of widely distant tribes.

In deciding questions of war, the Hasinais sometimes resorted to prognostication and divination. Says Espinosa:

When they go to war, they hold general assemblies in the house of a chief and give drinks to one of those considered most valiant, until he loses or pretends to lose, consciousness. After a day and a night he says that he has seen where the enemy were and whether or not they were prepared, and they predict their pretended victories accordingly. They do the same enroute when they go their journeys, and with a fox's tail they make an astrolobe by means of which to see future events.[2]

It is not clear what this astrolobe was like.

One witness reported what he thought to be a prewar demonstration by the women, demanding vengeance for the death of husbands, brothers, and friends. In a body, and accompanied by armed warriors, they entered the cabins of the chief men and, weeping, chanted lugubrious prayers for the scalps of their enemies.[3] Another witness tells us that war ceremonies were held at the large assembly or town house, and that after they began, the warriors taking part did not re-enter their own dwellings before departing for the campaign. Mean-

[1] Fray Francisco Jesús María de Casañas, Relación, August 15, 1691, AGN, Historia, vol. 394, fol. 6; Pierre Margry, ed. and trans., *Découvertes et établissements des français dans le sud de l'Amérique Septentrionale, 1614–1754* 3: 354, 355; Isidro Felix de Espinosa, *Chrónica apostólica, y seráphica de todos los colegios de propaganda fide de esta Nueva-España*, pp. 436–37.

[2] Espinosa, *Chrónica*, p. 430.

[3] Michel described this ceremony as enacted among the Kadohadachos, but says that he had seen it before on the way, doubtless among Hasinais during their preparations for the Canohatinno war. Margry, ed. and trans., *Découvertes*, 3: 410.

Earthenware pipe, natural size, taken from a burial site on Mrs. Emma Owens's farm, Anderson County, Texas. Courtesy Texas Archeological Research Lab (neg. no. 41An21-7), University of Texas, Austin.

while the women prepared the food for the assembled war-riors, and the youths served the leading men.[4]

For several days before the Canohatinno war the leading men trained the youth to run and shoot. One of the exercises consisted of running between two stakes, "*a que l'emporteroit*

[4] Ibid., p. 354. Massanet, describing the Nabedache assembly house, evidently notes a similar custom, saying that while the "chiefs" were in session they were fed by the "governor" (the Nabedache chief) and served by their "pages." See: "Damián Massanet, "Carta de Don Damian Mazanet a Don Carlos de Siguenza y Gongora Sobre el Descubrimiento de la Bahia de Espiritu Santo," trans. Lilia Casis, *Quarterly* of the Texas State Historical Association 2 (April, 1899): 304.

Indian burial found on the Emma Owens Farm, Anderson County, adjacent to Caddo Creek. The burial was excavated by a University of Texas crew in 1931. Seven large conch shell beads were discovered in the loose dirt left by earlier digging, but none were found in place around the skeleton. A badly rusted metal knife (or dagger blade) was between the right shoulder and chin, with the point sticking downward. Next to the knife was a flint awl or drill. A paint stone was found at the outer part of the right arm. At the left shoulder was a badly decayed mussel shell and next to it a cone-shaped pipe. One the left shoulder near the chin was a small pot bearing the "sun symbol" design. Courtesy, Texas Archeological Research Lab. (Neg. no. 41 An 21-4), University of Texas, Austin.

de vitesse dans plus ou moins de tours."[5] A popular festival held in May, which suggested to Espinosa the European Maypole, seems to have been regarded as a special training for military exploits. Here too the most conspicuous feature was the running contest. In the midst of a prairie was set a tall pine sapling, stripped of its bark, with only the topmost boughs remaining. Around this pole a wide curved or circular path was cleared, and at sunrise on the morning of the appointed day the men began their running race, the test apparently being that of endurance. Says Espinosa, "The day is very celebrated among all [of them] because it serves as a test of arbitrary [?] to run when they fight with their enemies."[6]

Espinosa describes the same kind of running exercise, in the form of a contest, participated by young men, boys, and even girls, during the September festival and states that it was regarded as a form of training for war:

All of the same age or size being in a line, at the signal to go they all run at the top of their speed and turn at a tree, which is perhaps a musket shot away, and return to where they started. They continue two or three rounds and then give up. Then the [smaller] boys and girls do the same in a proportionate way. . . . All the relatives observe very carefully who is the victor, and this one bears the laurels . . . for those who fall behind or tire out without finishing the race, their wives and relatives raise a doleful howl, for, they say, when they go to war, being slow, they will either be imprisoned, captured, or killed by their enemies. This lasts sometimes more than an hour.[7]

Casañas thus describes some of the ceremonies, seen by him presumably, preceding an important campaign: For a week or more the warriors, assembled in their war paints, feasted, danced, and performed religious rites to propitiate the spirits. To effect the latter aim, offerings were brought of meat, maize, bows, arrows, tobacco, *acoixo* [an herb], and the fat of buffalo

[5]Margry, ed. and trans., *Découvertes*, 3: 353–54. See also Espinosa, *Chrónica*, on running exercises.
[6]Espinosa, *Chrónica*, p. 434.
[7]Ibid., p. 433.

heart, and portions of these things were hung upon a pole in front of the dancers. Before the pole there was a fire and sitting near it a priest dressed "like a demon." From time to time he burned incense of tobacco and the fat of buffalo heart. As he did so each warrior approached the fire and rubbed himself with the smoke, "thinking" says the narrator, "that thereby God would grant him what he asked." At other times the priest took a lighted brand and covered the offerings with fumes of the burning buffalo fat. In the intervals between the dances a person stepped forth and in oratorical tones instructed the warriors what to ask for during the next dance. Their petitions were directed primarily toward vengeance on the enemy and success in the approaching campaign. They asked Caddi Ayo to grant death to many enemies, swiftness of foot, or valor to resist. They addressed fire, water, air, maize, animals, or whatnot, asking each to grant its particular favor. On the last day of the meeting the caddi delivered an exhortation inciting the braves to valor and charging them to let no family ties deter them from going.[8]

Such were some of the preliminary ceremonies, as seen and understood by our early witnesses. While the warriors were absent, the women made tearful demonstration, continuing the supplication of the spirits.[9]

Victory Ceremonies

The victorious return from a campaign was celebrated by prolonged public festivities, the bestowal of honors upon the successful warriors, and horrible tortures for the unfortunate captives. Below is given the substance of Joutel's account of the public demonstrations attending the victorious return of a party of Hasinais from the Canohatinno war. How much it is colored to make a good story, students of Indian ceremonial may be able to determine.

[8] Casañas, Relación, fol. 6.
[9] Margry, ed. and trans., Découvertes, 3: 375.

While the warriors were absent on this campaign Joutel was surprised one morning at day-break to see a troupe of women enter his cabin with their faces and bodies disfigured with paints. They chanted awhile in gutteral tones, then danced hand in hand in a ring. From time to time they took the scalps that were hanging in the lodge and cut figures in the air with them, especially presenting them first to one side and then another, "as if to mock the tribes from whom the scalps had been taken." The ceremony lasted two or three hours. Joutel afterwards learned, he said, that it was a method of feminine rejoicing at the news of a victory won by their husbands and brothers.[10]

Now the women set to work to prepare food to carry to the returning warriors. Next day they set out to meet them, and that night the victors entered the village with scalps, skulls, and captives. One prisoner had been scalped alive and sent to her friends bearing as a threat a charge of powder and shot solicited from the French. Another woman captive was delivered before entering the village to the Hasinai women to become the victim of their savage rage and cruelty. Armed with clubs and sharpened sticks they set upon her for the preliminary torture. After this prelude, one pulled out a handful of her hair, another cut off a finger, and a third thrust out an eye. Then the coup de grace was given with more furious blows and thrusts. Finally they cut up her body and preserved the pieces to be fed to prisoners of the victim's tribe.[11]

Next morning there began a celebration which lasted three days. First the twenty most successful warriors went to the house of the chief and then to the houses of other leading men, where they were honored by a ceremony that might be compared with that of conferring knighthood. It seems to have been repeated at each of the leading houses. The de-

[10] Ibid.

[11] Joutel did not see this torture, but it was described to him, he said, by some of his companions who were eyewitnesses. Of forty-eight persons captured, quarter was given only to two women and some children. Margry, ed. and trans., *Découvertes*, 3: 377–78.

scription following is that of its performance at the house where Joutel was staying. Seated on mats were the chief men of the village. An old man who had not been to the war acted as master of ceremonies, which he opened with a long harangue. Next each successful brave, in his turn, bearing a bow and two arrows, and preceded first by a woman with a long reed and a deerskin and then by his wife bearing the scalp he had taken, marched before the company. The brave handed the scalp to the orator, who, while delivering a harangue, thrust it out north, south, east, and west, and then placed it upon the mat. After the ceremony had been repeated for each warrior, another long harangue followed, and then a feast and tobacco were served by the women to the assembled crowd. During the feast the master of ceremonies offered food and tobacco to the scalps, while the youthful captives taken in the recent battle were forced to eat pieces of the tortured woman's body.[12]

It was at this ceremony, possibly, that the warriors who had taken scalps were, according to Casañas, given a distinctive name. He tells us that such were called *ay mayoya,* meaning "great man," and that their "coat of arms" consisted of the scalps they had taken.[13]

War Methods

The Hasinai caddi went to war with the rest, but the elective war chiefs were more usually the leaders of the various bands. Women were also taken along, as servants and to help carry back plunder.[14]

The Hasinais followed the usual Indian method of warfare, fighting in small parties and depending more upon surprise attacks and swiftness in retreat than upon superior skill or

[12] Ibid., pp. 379–81. The Talons and Casañas also mention the dances following a victory and the honors bestowed upon the takers of the most scalps. Ibid., p. 616.

[13] Casañas, Relación, fol. 8.

[14] Ibid.; Margry, ed. and trans., *Découvertes,* 3: 378.

strength.[15] Quarter for the adult male enemy was the exception, but women and children were regularly spared to be sold or kept as wives and servants.[16] When first seen by the French in 1687 the Hasinais had Canohatinno slaves, and in later years they maintained with the French a regular trade in Apache captives.

When the Spaniards first came to settle among them, the Hasinais had a few horses, but probably they did not use them extensively for war purposes, although in 1687 they supplied mounts for six Frenchmen who joined them in the Canohatinno war.[17] Within a quarter of a century they usually went to war on horseback. They made bridles and bits of horsehair, and saddles of folded buckskin, with wooden stirrups suspended by horsehair and probably by buffalo hide strings.[18] The buffalo hide quiver full of arrows was swung at the warrior's back by a shoulder strap.

Scalping the enemy was a common Hasinai practice. Says Pierre Talon "they remove the skin of the head together with the hair, which they dry and fill with grass. Each guards those he has been able to raise in order to make trophies of them. They hang them on canes on the top of their cabins and, when displaying them, raise them aloft in their hands with much pomp and ostentation."[19] When there were several to share honors for the taking of a single scalp, they divided it, and twisted the separate locks spirally around a reed, each portion taking rank with an entire scalp.[20] Different tribes of Indians had different methods of removing the scalp of the enemy. We are told that the Hasinai cut it from the forehead to the ears.[21]

Not alone the scalps but sometimes the heads or skulls of

[15] Margry, ed. and trans., *Découvertes*, 3: 616.
[16] Ibid., pp. 354, 378–81.
[17] Benjamin F. French, ed., *Historical Collection of Louisiana*, 4: 204.
[18] Margry, ed. and trans., *Découvertes*, 5: 502.
[19] Ibid., 3: 616.
[20] Ibid., p. 364.
[21] Ibid., p. 376.

the enemy also were brought home as trophies.[22] After being duly displayed in the victory ceremonies, they were carried to the lodge of the Chenesi and hung on a pole or tree outside.[23] When they had been allowed to hang there for some time, they were buried with elaborate ceremonial, which Espinósa describes as follows:

For this purpose the men and women gather on an appointed night at the place where the skulls are and make a number of fires. The lugubrious and doleful instruments being prepared and the singers and the chapel being arranged, seated on the ground, smutted with coal, and with head bowed, they sing in time with doleful voice. Then, covered from head to feet with skins, they dance without moving from one spot, the women in a file and apart from the men. This lasts the greater part of the night. Then a decrepit old man and a following of strong young men ranged round the tree where the skulls are hung, with an arrow in the hand and facing one of the cardinal points, shout or cry out. Then they turn to the other cardinal points and do likewise. From time to time they fire a gun toward the skulls, and all together raise to the *traguido* a confused shout. The next morning they daub their faces and arms with earth and carry the skulls for burial to the ash heap near the fire temple, where they spend the remainder of the day in various ceremonies. The whole performance appears like an affair of Inferno—both the singing and the paraphernalia they display. They offer to the skulls ground pinole and other food, which are eaten instead by the living after they finish their prayers and superstitious ceremonies.[24]

Cannibalism

Cannibalism among the American Indians, though usually regarded as ceremonial rather than economic in its significance, was quite widespread. Among many tribes parts of the bodies of captured foes were eaten in "the belief that bravery and

---

[22] Casañas, Relación, fol. 8; Espinosa, *Chrónica*, p. 433.
[23] "Los Calaberas los tiene el gran Xinesi corca de su Casa Colgadas en un Arbol"; Casañas, Relación, fol. 8; Espinosa, *Chrónica*, 433.
[24] Espinosa, *Chrónica*, pp. 424, 434.

other desirable qualities of an enemy would pass, through actual ingestion of a part of his body, into that of the consumer."[25]

Penicaut, who, to be sure, has a well-deserved reputation for romancing, in 1714 reported among the Hasinais an altogether credible case of cannibalism coupled with torture and ceremonial. While he was at one of their villages, he said, 150 warriors returned with two Kitaesches (Kichai) whom they had captured in the campaign just finished. To dispose of them two scaffolds were erected on the prairie nearby, and on each a captive was suspended by his hands and with his feet above the ground. For half an hour at night and again in the morning, they were kept thus, each time facing the sun. In the morning the people gathered on the spot, built fires, and heated pots of water, while four old men made incisions in the bodies of the captives, caught their blood, and carried it to two other elders, who cooked it and gave it to the women and children to drink. The victims having expired, their bodies were placed upon a platform and cut up into bits which were distributed among the villagers and stewed in the boiling pots. Meanwhile the people danced, and when the flesh was cooked they ate it.[26] This account of Penicaut's is apparently verified in an ambiguous passage by Casañas, a much more trustworthy witness. Summing up the cruelties of the Hasinais toward their enemies he says: "Finally, in this they do not manifest more harshness than that shown by their enemies; that is, tying their hands and feet to a pole like a cross, and when there, cutting off pieces, drinking the blood, and eating the flesh half cooked." From the context it seems that Casañas is describing the Hasinai custom rather than that of their enemies.[27]

[25] Frederick Webb Hodge, ed., *Handbook of the American Indians North of Mexico*, Bureau of American Ethnology Bulletin 30 (1907), 1: 201.

[26] Margry, ed. and trans., *Découvertes*, 5: 503–504. It is doubtful that he was among the Hasinais at this time. Certainly he did not go with St. Denis on the occasion as he claimed.

[27] Casañas, Relación, fols. 12–13.

Bibliography

NOTE: This bibliography has been constructed from the foot-notes in the original manuscript, supplemented with sources cited in the Editor's Introduction (see "Editor's Sources" below).

PRIMARY SOURCES

Spanish Documents

Archivo General de la Nación (AGN), Mexico City; microfilm in the Bancroft Library.
Bexar Archives, University of Texas, Austin; originals and microfilm.
Nacogdoches Archives, State Library, Austin, Texas.
National Anthropological Archives, Smithsonian Institution, Washington, D.C.

Books (Firsthand Accounts)

Bandelier, Fanny, trans. *The Journey of Álvar Núñez Cabeza de Vaca and His Companions from Florida to the Pacific, 1528–1536.* New York: A. S. Barnes, 1905.
Espinosa, R. P., Fr. Isidro Felix de. *Chrónica apostólica, y seráphica de todos los colegios de propaganda fide de esta Nueva-Espana, de Missioneros Franciscanos observantas: Erigidos con authoridad pontifica, y regia, para la reformaciones de los fieles, y conversion de los gentiles.* Mexico City: Hogal, 1746.
French, Benjamin F. *Historical Collections of Louisiana.* 5 vols. New York: Wiley and Putnam, 1846–53.
Margry, Pierre. *Découvertes et établissements des français dans l'ouest et dans le sud de l'Amérique Septentrionale, 1614–1754.* 6 vols. Paris: D. Jouaust, 1879–88.
Rivera y Villalón, Pedro de. *Diario y Derrotero de lo caminado, visita, . . . de Nueva España.* Guatemala City: Sebastian de Arbalo, 1736.
Smith, Buckingham, ed. *Documentos para la historia de la Florida y tierra adyacentes.* 5 vols. London: Trübner, 1857.

Winship, George Parker, trans. *The Coronado Expedition, 1540–1542.* Fourteenth Annual Report of the Bureau of American Ethnology (1892–93). Washington, D.C.: U.S. Government Printing Office, 1896.

Articles (Firsthand Accounts)

Ayer, Mrs. Edward E., trans. "Benavides's Memorial, 1630." *Land of Sunshine* 14 (1901): 39–52.

Bonilla, Antonio. "Bonilla's Brief Compendium of the History of Texas, 1772." Translated by Elizabeth W. West., *Quarterly* of the Texas State Historical Association 8 (July, 1904): 3–78.

Massanet, Damián. "Carta de Don Damian Mazanet a Don Carlos de Siguenza y Góngora Sobre el descubrimiento de la Bahia de Espiritu Santo." Translated by Lilia M. Casis, *Quarterly* of the Texas State Historical Association 2 (April, 1899): 253–312.

SECONDARY SOURCES

Books

Clark, Robert C. *The Beginnings of Texas, 1684–1718.* Austin: University of Texas Press, 1907.

Dorsey, George A. *Traditions of the Caddo.* Washington, D.C.: Carnegie Institution, 1905.

Dorsey, J. Owen. *Omaha Sociology.* Third Annual Report of the Bureau of American Ethnology. Washington, D.C.: U.S. Government Printing Office, 1884.

Farrand, Livingston. *Basis of American History, 1500–1900.* New York: Harper & Bros., 1904.

Hodge, Frederick Webb, ed. *Handbook of American Indians North of Mexico.* Bulletin No. 30 of the Bureau of American Ethnology. 2 vol. Washington, D.C.: U.S. Government Printing Office, 1907–10.

Hoffman, Walter J. *The Menomini Indians.* Fourteenth Annual Report of the Bureau of American Ethnology. Washington, D.C.: U.S. Government Printing Office, 1896.

Mooney, James. *The Ghost-Dance Religion.* Fourteenth Annual Report of the Bureau of American Ethnology. Washington, D.C.: U.S. Government Printing Office, 1896.

Powell, J. W. *Indian Linguistic Families of America North of Mexico.* Seventh Annual Report of the Bureau of American Ethnology.

Washington, D.C.: U.S. Government Printing Office, 1891.

―――― *Wyandot Government*. First Annual Report of the Bureau of American Ethnology. Washington, D.C.: U.S. Government Printing Office, 1881.

Yarrow, H. C. *A Further Contribution to the Study of Mortuary Customs of the North American Indians*. First Annual Report of the Bureau of American Ethnology. Washington, D.C.: U.S. Government Printing Office, 1881.

Articles

Bolton, Herbert E. "The Founding of Mission Rosario: A Chapter in the History of the Gulf Coast." *Quarterly* of the Texas State Historical Association 10 (October, 1906): 113–39.

―――― "The Native Tribes About the East Texas Missions." *Quarterly* of the Texas State Historical Association 11 (April, 1908): 249–76.

―――― "The Old Stone Fort at Nacogdoches." *Quarterly* of the Texas State Historical Association 9 (October, 1905): 283–85.

Carr, Lucien. "On the Social and Political Position of Women Among the Huron-Iroquois Tribes." *Reports of the Peabody Museum* 3 (1880–86): 207–59.

Clark, Robert C. "The Beginnings of Texas." *Quarterly* of the Texas State Historical Association 5 (January, 1902): 171–205.

―――― "Louis Juchereau de Saint-Denis and the Reestablishment of the Tejas Missions." *Quarterly* of the Texas State Historical Association 6 (July, 1902): 1–26.

Dunbar, John B. "The Pawnee Indians: Their History and Ethnology." *Magazine of American History* 4 (April, 1880): 241–81.

Gatschet, Albert S. "The Karankawa Indians." *Archaeological and Ethnological Papers of the Peabody Museum* 1 (1891): 21–103.

Harby, Mrs. Lee C. "The Earliest Texas." *Annual Report* of the American Historical Association. Washington, D.C.: U.S. Government Printing Office, 1892, 195–205.

―――― "The Tejas: Their Habits, Government, and Superstitions." In *Annual Report* of the American Historical Association. Washington, D.C.: U.S. Government Printing Office, 1895, pp. 63–82.

Henshaw, Henry W. "Popular Fallacies Respecting the Indians." *American Anthropologist* 7 (January–March, 1905): 104–13.

Kenney, M. M. "Tribal Society Among Texas Indians." *Quarterly* of the Texas State Historical Association 1 (July, 1897): 26–33.

Morgan, Lewis H. "House and House-Life of the American Aborigines." *Contributions to North American Ethnology* 4. Washington, D.C.: U.S. Government Printing Office, 1881.

Ponton, Miss Brownie, and Bates M. M'Farland. "Álvar Nuñez Cabeza de Vaca: A Preliminary Report on His Wanderings in Texas." *Quarterly* of the Texas State Historical Association 1 (January, 1898): 166–86.

Schimidt, Edmond J. P. "Louis Juchereau de Saint-Denis and the Re-Establishment of the Tejas Mission." *Quarterly* of the Texas State Historical Association 6 (July, 1902): 1–26.

——— "Ven. María Jesús de Agreda: A Correction." *Quarterly* of the Texas State Historical Association 1 (October, 1897): 121–24.

Zavala, A. de. "Religious Beliefs of the Tejas or Hasinai Indians." *Publications* of the Texas Folklore Society 1 (1916): 39–43.

Editor's Sources

PRIMARY SOURCES

Bannon, John F. "The Hasinai Manuscript of Herbert Eugene Bolton." September 9, 1978. In the possession of the editor.

Bolton, Herbert Eugene. Bolton Papers. Bancroft Library, University of California, Berkeley. Part 2. Bolton's Correspondence, 1906–1950.

——— "How I Got That Way." Paper in the Bolton Papers. Part 2. Bancroft Library, University of California, Berkeley.

National Anthropological Archives, Smithsonian Institution. Files containing correspondence between Bolton, Frederick W. Hodge, W. H. Holmes, and John R. Swanton.

Spier, Leslie. Papers. Department of Anthropology, University of California, Berkeley.

SECONDARY SOURCES

Bannon, John Francis, ed. *Bolton and the Spanish Borderlands.* Norman: University of Oklahoma Press, 1964.

——— "Herbert E. Bolton, His *Guide* in Making." *Southwestern Historical Quarterly* 73 (July, 1969): 35–55.

————. *Herbert Eugene Bolton: The Historian and the Man.* Tucson, University of Arizona Press, 1978.

Bolton, Herbert Eugene. "De Los Mapas." *Quarterly* of the Texas State Historical Association 6 (July, 1902): 69–70.

————. "The Native Tribes About the East Texas Missions." *Quarterly* of the Texas State Historical Association 11 (April, 1908): 249–76.

————. "Some Materials for Southwestern History in the Archivo de Mexico." *Quarterly* of the Texas State Historical Association 6 (October, 1902): 103–12, and 7 (January, 1904): 196–213.

————. "The Spanish Abandonment and Re-Occupation of East Texas, 1773–1779." *Quarterly* of the Texas State Historical Association 9 (October, 1905): 67–137.

————. "Tienda de Cuervo's Ynspección of Laredo, 1757." Quarterly of the Texas State Historical Association 6 (January, 1903): 187–203.

Griffith, William J. *The Hasinai Indians of East Texas as Seen by Europeans, 1687–1772.* Tulane University Publication, No. 12. New Orleans: Middle America Research Institute, 1954.

Hammond, George P. "Herbert Eugene Bolton, 1870–1953.' *Americas* 9 (April, 1953): 392.

McHugh, Tom. *The Time of the Buffalo.* New York: Alfred A. Knopf, 1972.

Magnaghi, Russell. "Herbert E. Bolton and Sources for American Indian Studies." *Western Historical Quarterly* 6 (January, 1975): 33–46.

Swanton, John R. *Indian Tribes of the Lower Mississippi Valley and Adjacent Coast of the Gulf of Mexico.* Bureau of American Ethnology Bulletin No. 43. Washington, D.C.: U.S. Government Printing Office, 1911.

Wilmsen, Edwin N. "A Suggested Developmental Sequence for House Forms in the Caddoan Area." *Bulletin* of the Texas Archaeological Society 30 (1959): 35–50.

Index